CW01186735

Muddy Spuds

Muddy Spuds

Shona Pollock

First published in Great Britain in 2021 by Jersey Royals Publishing

Copyright © Shona Pollock 2021

Shona Pollock has asserted her right under the Copyright, Designs and Patents Act 1988 to be identified as the author of this work.

Illustrations and cover by Harriet Hodgkinson

Author Photograph © 2021 Mark Hodgkinson

All rights reserved. No part of this publication may be reproduced, stored in a retrieval system or transmitted, in any form or by any means, without the publisher's prior permission in writing.

This book is sold subject to the condition that it shall not, by way of trade or otherwise, be lent, resold, hired out or otherwise circulated without the publisher's prior consent in any form of binding or cover other than that in which it is published and without a similar condition, including this condition, being imposed on the subsequent purchaser.

DISCLAIMER: Cooking and eating involve inherent dangers. Please undertake only activities that you believe to be safe and comfortable. Shona Pollock and Jersey Royals Publishing assume no responsibility or liability for any damages you may experience as a result of following these recipes. All dietary indications in the recipes are a starting point for your own review, not an absolute statement of vegetarian, dairy-free or alcohol-free status.

Edited, designed and produced by Tandem Publishing
http://tandempublishing.yolasite.com

ISBN: 978-1-3999-0089-8

10 9 8 7 6 5 4 3 2 1

A CIP catalogue record for this book is available from the British Library.

Printed and bound in Great Britain by CPI Group (UK) Ltd,
Croydon CR0 4YY.

'For Mimi and Max'

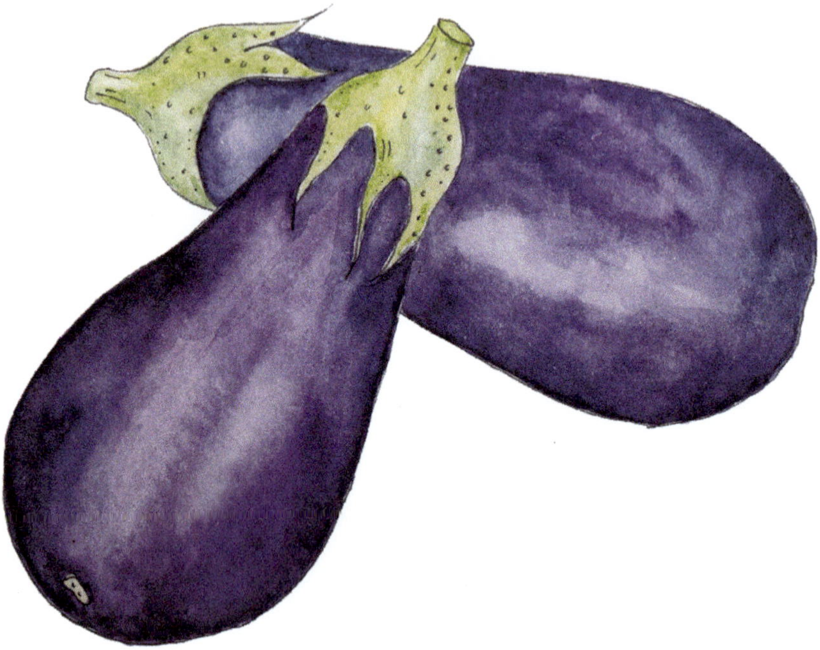

Contents

Introduction	ix
Rules	xv
Canapés	1
Starters	17
Sides & Salads	51
Fish	83
Chicken	99
Pork	131
Beef & Lamb	141
General Meat Cooking Times	*152*
Game, Duck & Guinea Fowl	171
Sauces	183
Vegetarian	191
Puddings	209
Cakes & Baking	259
Christmas & Delicious Drinks	283
Acknowledgements	295
Suppliers	297
Index	299

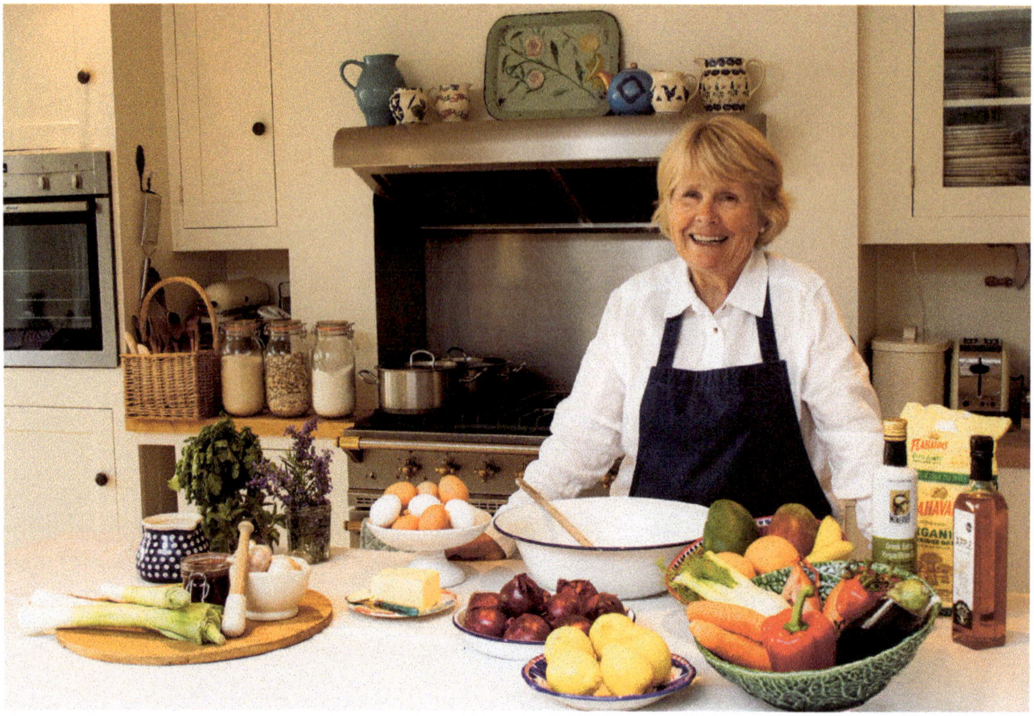

Introduction

For ages I have wanted to put all my favourite recipes into a book to hand down to my son Max, my nephews Alexander, Rory, Joe, Tommie and Ned, and my niece Lucy. My other niece Mimi used to love helping me cook; sadly we lost her in a dreadful snowboarding accident in Chamonix in 2012. She had made me the most beautiful chocolate truffles a couple of weeks before she left for the Alps, and you will find the recipe later in the book – I never forget returning from a job to find both kitchen and Mimi's face covered in the best cocoa powder from the ingredients cupboard.

Cooking for me is a pleasure and my favourite hobby – I have an enthusiasm to get food right and tasting delicious.

I also believe in the right food at the right place at the right time. We used to go to Corfu every summer, where I discovered some truly excellent local restaurants – many right by the sea. I couldn't bear it when I saw British families there ordering steak with pepper sauce for their children, when right there you have the most delicious fresh fish every day. I also shudder when I go to the mountains and find oysters on the menu in restaurants – surely not! There can be nothing nicer than sitting by the fire at home in the winter and having a bowl of stew and mash with lightly sautéed cabbage, and then in the summer sitting outside and having chicken on the barbecue with new potatoes and salad.

I really try to stick to seasonal food – I do my best to persuade my Brides and Grooms not to have asparagus and strawberries in the winter. Sometimes, of course, I have to give in – after all, it is their day.

I believe that good food depends on the best ingredients simply cooked. I don't think of myself as a 'chef' – I am a *cook*, and a lover of eating. I don't think you have to be innovative to be a competent cook. Often people try so hard to do something completely different, and the result is almost inedible. Watching Rick Stein the other day, he mentioned that in this country we lack family-run home-cooking restaurants – like they have in Greece, Italy and Spain and many other countries – and I couldn't agree more. There used to be many in France, but sadly where we go nowadays many have closed down or changed with a menu to suit more international tastes than local traditional recipes.

My early memories of loving food go back to when I was quite small with my family. We were brought up in Jersey in the Channel Islands and our holidays were spent bobbing around in the Channel in my father's little sailing boat. We headed for Saint-Malo in Brittany and spent the whole journey looking forward to eating things like langoustine, praires farcies and wonderful French bread (which you could not get our side of the Channel in those days). I remember the day my sister and I first tasted proper homemade mayonnaise there with a delicious lobster dinner – so different to the salad cream back home we had been used to. My father always liked us to eat fish next to the sea, but sometimes we would have the most magnificent steak and chips with garlic butter at the Duchess Anne, a restaurant which is still there where a photograph of my father and godparents still hangs sixty years later – all with fags in one hand and a glass of wine in the other. I remember always wanting to bring a baguette home on the boat with us but my father said it would go stale in a few hours and how right he was.

At home dinners were always special, albeit a bit formal, with the best ingredients cooked for each occasion. My father's favourite dish to cook, as I remember, was a really delicious buttery roast chicken with lots of crispy chips – I wish I knew how he did them. He also used to barbecue a wonderful steak accompanied by a crispy salad with my stepmother's mustardy French dressing. I have put the recipe in this book but it has never tasted quite the same as when I was a child.

The other thing I remember so well as a child was my father's garden – he had a large garden with several gardeners coming in to help. There was an asparagus bed, and he reckoned that asparagus had to be cooked almost as soon as it was picked, and I clearly recall him there in the garden, having set up a camping stove and big pot of boiling water, into which he threw the large, delicious stems straight from the ground. I have never been able to buy asparagus out of season in supermarkets since!

At home we all used to celebrate certain things together – for example the first Jersey Royal new potato, with lots of Jersey butter, and the first strawberry of the season was always marked with a 'wish'. To this day, I still insist on buying a sack of muddy spuds for any event I cater for – much to the dismay of my kitchen assistants who are tasked with scrubbing them clean! Their taste is so much richer and superior to the ready-washed potatoes one can buy so easily.

In a nutshell, I just love to cook, whether it is for my clients or for friends and family at home. I love going to food shops and interesting supermarkets and food halls! As a child, once a year we were allowed to go to Harrods with a 10-shilling note in our pockets (50p nowadays) and my treat was to go to the food department and spend it there.

I know people think I am unusual as I really do not enjoy going to fancy restaurants; it seems to me that there they worry more about how the food looks than how it tastes. My idea of heaven is to go to the River Café where they do not serve foams and odd things, just delicious simple ingredients cooked to perfection. I could list several simple restaurants in London which don't try to be pretentious or get away with serving not particularly good food on a square plate at an inflated price.

As a family we go skiing whenever we can to the same resort,

Méribel in France, and it has become our second home. Whereas most people would spend hours talking about which run they like the most, my sister and I spend the weeks prior to the holiday discussing where we are going to have lunch and what we are going to eat at each restaurant. Sadly, the restaurants there are no longer as simple as they used to be. When we first were in Méribel some forty-five years ago we used to ski over to Val Thorens for the day, heading to the only restaurant there – Bar de la Marine (still there but not the same) where all they served was a huge Pot-au-Feu, which the patron would have bubbling gently over a fire all day long, standing stirring it with a cigarette in his mouth. We salivated about it all the way up and down the pistes on our three-hour journey to Val Thorens. Our other favourite restaurant, also still there, is Bel Air in Courchevel 1650, which has on its menu a wonderful salad of lovely soft lettuce leaves, grated Gruyère and walnuts with a wonderful mustardy dressing – I hope they never change it. Whilst on the subject of restaurants in Méribel I have to mention the Télébar, which still serves the delicious Veal à la Crème and the best chips I have ever tasted.

As a young girl I adored cookery lessons at school, where we made fairy cakes and biscuits – these lessons stopped with a greater focus on academia. When I left school, I wanted to go and learn to cook but, in those days, it just wasn't considered a career so off I went and did bilingual secretarial training and went on to work as a secretary at which I was mostly bored silly and probably not very good!

My cooking career started after I had worked in events at a company called IMG for about eight years. Towards the end of my working life there I organised all the housing for tennis players during the two weeks of Wimbledon, and part of my job was to employ cooks/chefs for the players. I had a wonderful time but started envying the cooks I employed and realised that was what I wanted to do.

To cut a long story short, I went from cooking for people at Wimbledon and The Open Golf to doing lots of hospitality at the BBC and even catering for the Spice Girls when they started out as a girl band. I now have a reasonable-sized catering company and we specialise in weddings; pre-Covid we were doing about forty or so lovely weddings a year.

Over the years, along with my team of excellent chefs (Paul, Liz, Wiz and Nat), we have tried and tested so many recipes and worked with really wonderful clients that now, over this unusual lockdown period, I thought I would create a book to record the best of them.

My team of waiters/waitresses have all been with me for ages and they, also, have many stories to tell. There is almost nobody Mary has not served – she has banked so many marvellous stories (nearly all nice) about people from the Queen Mother and Princess Margaret to Richard Branson, to name a few.

I love food shopping and wish we had food markets like they have in France – they are just perfect and I am afraid the farmers' markets in London are just not the same. I live in Barnes in South West London and am fortunate enough to have a wonderful vegetable and fruit shop, Two Peas In A Pod, run and owned by Malcolm, a delicious fish shop run and owned by Michael and an excellent cheese shop, run and owned by Jill and Valentina. There used to be a proper family butcher, Seals, which sadly sold up, so now I use a very good butcher in Chiswick called Mackens, run by Rodney for whom nothing is too much trouble. I buy my sourdough from Gail's in Barnes, which we are so lucky to have here.

You will see from the recipe introductions that many of them are old family friends, coming from various members of my extended family, but also from the amazing cookery school I attended in the early 1970s. There are also many which we have simply developed over the years with my lovely team, in the kitchen, just chatting recipes and ideas through. Some are assembled from my collection of old newspaper and magazine cuttings and others were originally given to me by clients who have requested a specific favourite for their main course at a wedding. The origins of some of these recipes are now lost, but I'm very grateful to all who have contributed. Of one thing I'm sure: all are good and well tried and tested.

— Shona Pollock, 2021

Conversion Table

Throughout the recipes I have put an oven temperature in Celsius for a fan-assisted oven, as I find most houses I cook in have one. If you are using a static electric oven add another 20 degrees to the temperature control – for example if I say 160°C just make it 180°C.

120°C	250°F	Mark 1
130°C	275°F	Mark 2
150°C	300°F	Mark 3
160°C	320°F	Mark 4
170°C	340°F	Mark 5
180°C	360°F	Mark 6
200°C	400°F	Mark 7
210°C	410°F	Mark 8
220°C	430°F	Mark 9

Rules

I have certain rules I try and stick to, and I know I drive the chefs who work for me mad. They will laugh when they see them here on paper, so here goes:

1. I do not like using stock cubes – I always make my own stock, as we usually have chicken carcasses left over it is so easy to bubble them away on the stove with some onions, carrots, celery, black peppercorns and bay leaf and a good bit of Maldon salt. If I don't have any fresh stock I prefer just adding water and maybe some extra seasoning.

2. I don't like ready ground black pepper or ready ground nutmeg – it is like sawdust. I also don't like those huge jars of ground spices as I feel they go off so quickly unless you are going to get through them pretty fast.

3. I never add alcohol to cooking without reducing it first, other than something like a sweet wine in a pudding recipe. If you want a slug of wine in gravy I would reduce it first as otherwise it overpowers the taste.

4. I never use half-fat things – I would rather eat less of full-fat yoghurt than have to put up with horrid half-fat yoghurts, cream cheeses or creams etc. I do, however, like to drink semi-skimmed milk but would never use it in cooking – always full fat for me.

5. I do think using good margarine like Flora or Vitalite makes good cakes, although I would never use it in pastry.

6. I never use artificial sweeteners – artificial sweetener is very bad for you and leaves a horrible after-taste in any recipe.

7. I always use salted butter, but this is a personal preference.

8. Only use extra-virgin olive oil for drizzling on food or a lovely dressing. Wonderful as a dip for bread, or to pour over a cooked piece of meat or fish at the last minute. Use light olive oil or vegetable oil for frying.

9. When following my recipes, you do need to be a bit flexible as I find cakes sometimes take a bit longer than the recipe says – so when the time is up, always have a skewer around and just pop it into the centre of the cake – if it comes out clean the cake is ready. If not, just pop the cake back in for 5 minutes, check again and do another 5 minutes if you need. Just keep cooking until the skewer comes clean. Ovens vary so much that it is always difficult to be precise.

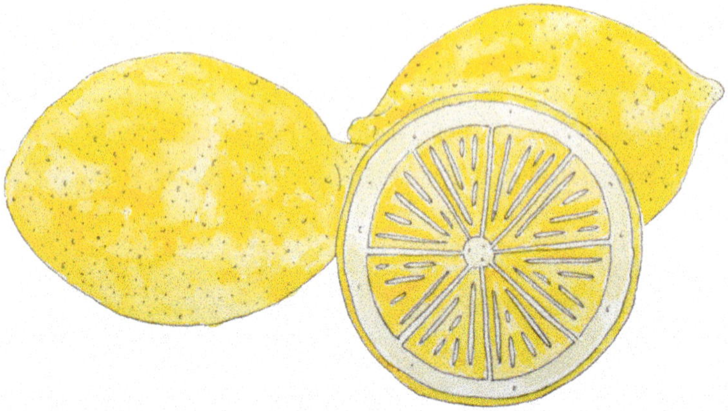

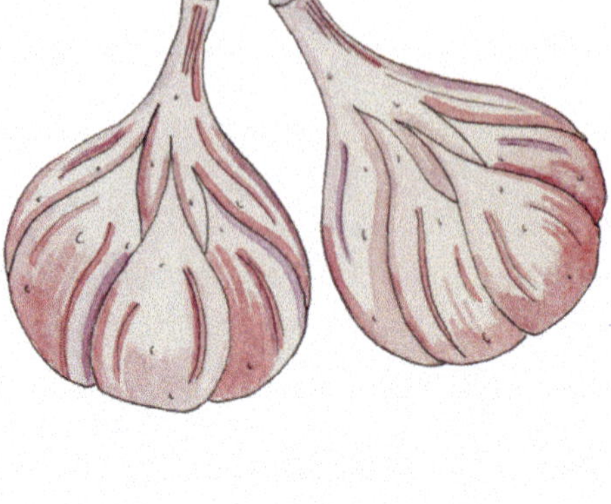

Canapés

Blinis

There are so many blini recipes but this is simple and works well – they also freeze well so you could make them on a rainy day and keep them in the freezer and just take out and top with crème fraîche and smoked salmon when you have friends around. They are particularly good with a teaspoon of horseradish cream added to the crème fraîche and topped with a nice sprig of dill. If you can't be bothered to go to the faff of making these you could always buy a packet of Scotch pancakes from a supermarket and stamp out (with a 4cm round pastry cutter/stamper) to use as bases – the sweetness of the pancake goes very well with the salmon and horseradish cream.

Makes 48

75g buckwheat flour
35g plain flour
1½ teaspoons baking powder
1 egg
180ml buttermilk
30g butter, melted

Sift flours and baking powder into a bowl with a teaspoon of salt.

Gradually whisk in egg, buttermilk and butter.

Cook the blinis in batches by dropping two teaspoons of batter into a large heated non-stick frying pan, turning the blinis until browned on both sides.

Bruschetta with Broad Beans, Pecorino & Mint Oil

Make this early in the bean season in June so their green skins are still soft and you can leave the skins on. You can use fresh or frozen peas instead but if using frozen beans you definitely have to remove the skins. You could either serve them as a starter or as a snack/canapé with drinks before dinner. I did these the other day for a wedding tasting and the Bride and Groom loved them – they were so impressed by the bright green colour of the pea and bean purée topped with the lovely pecorino and mint oil.

Makes 20

Preheat the oven to 170°C.

Slice baguette into very thin slices and toss in light olive oil and sea salt.

Bake in oven for about 5–10 minutes until brown and crisp – these will keep in an airtight container for ages.

Place 3 tablespoons of the oil and all the mint in a jug, season with salt and pepper and set aside.

Heat a large saucepan of water until boiling. Tip the beans or peas into the pan and bring back to the boil. This should take roughly 3–4 minutes.

Bruschetta
1 loaf of thin baguette (Gail's do a perfect one)

Topping
5 tablespoons light olive oil
1 sprig mint, leaves only, shredded
350g podded broad beans, or new baby broad beans, or peas
1 garlic clove, peeled
75g pecorino, shaved or grated coarsely
juice ½ lemon
salt and freshly ground black pepper

Drain and run under cold water, before setting about the slightly laborious job of slipping the broad beans, if using, out of their dull green skins.

Discard the skins and place the beans or peas in a food processor with the garlic, half the cheese, all the lemon juice and the remaining olive oil. Blend until you have a chunky paste, season with salt and pepper and taste, then season again if need be.

Spread this on the bruschetta and scatter with the remaining pecorino, drizzle everything with the mint oil and scatter over lots of black pepper.

Cheese Aigrettes

These make the most popular canapé, or you could serve 3 or 4 as a starter – only bore is you need to deep fry them which can cause a smell of frying in your kitchen – but they are so good I think they are worth the smell!
They are basically deep-fried cheese choux pastry. They are so much nicer than the recipe leads you to believe – I would say they are pretty much one of our favourite canapés we serve at a drinks party – especially for people who have had a few drinks – the lovely crisp outside is wonderful with the soft cheesy middle.

Boil the water and butter together, when bubbling draw aside and add the flour all at once.

Beat until smooth for about ½ minute then cool.

Beat in the eggs, one at a time, and continue to beat until the mixture is glossy-looking.

Stir in the cheese and season well with salt, pepper, and mustard.

Heat a pan of sunflower oil or rapeseed oil until a very faint blue haze rises from the surface. Drop in the mixture carefully, a teaspoonful at a time, allowing plenty of room for the mixture to rise. Increase the heat slightly and continue to fry the aigrettes for about 7 minutes or until well puffed up and golden brown. Lift out with a draining spoon, drain on soft paper, and dust with Parmesan.

Makes 20

¼ pint water
75g butter
80g plain flour
2 eggs
75g Gruyère or cheddar, finely diced
2 tablespoons grated Parmesan for dusting
1 litre of sunflower/rapeseed/vegetable oil

Crab Cakes

These are a very easy canapé to make – you could use fresh crab instead of a good tin of white crab meat but it is much more expensive and not really necessary in this particular recipe. We used to serve these in the Green Rooms at the BBC years ago when we did lots of post-production parties there – they were very popular hot or cold. You could also make them slightly larger and take them on a summer picnic.

Makes about 30

170g tin crab meat, drained
60ml mayonnaise
1 teaspoon lime zest
1 tablespoon chopped fresh coriander leaves
2 green shallots, finely chopped
70g stale breadcrumbs
1 egg, lightly beaten
1 tablespoon plain flour
vegetable oil for shallow-frying

Place crab meat on absorbent paper, squeeze out excess moisture.

Combine crab meat, mayonnaise, lime zest, coriander, shallots, breadcrumbs and egg in bowl.

Shape rounded teaspoons of the mixture into balls, flatten slightly, toss in flour.

Shallow-fry patties in batches in hot oil until lightly browned; drain.

Crunchy Thai Peanut Cakes

A canapé I think I reinvented from a very old recipe from an Australian Women's Weekly magazine years ago – it really is lovely but you must use chicken thighs liquidised and not chicken breasts as they are too dry. You can make the cakes, fry them and serve straight away. Alternatively, we have made, browned and then frozen them for a later date – they warm up well in a medium oven. You can leave the peanuts out if you have someone with a nut allergy, but they are not quite so good.

Dissolve the sugar in the soy sauce.

Put the chopped chicken thigh meat in the food processor with the sugar, soy sauce, sweet chilli sauce, peanuts, breadcrumbs, Thai curry paste, coriander and pulse until well mixed and soft.

Make the mixture into 24 small flat balls and refrigerate for 30 minutes before frying in a pan – once fried, drain on kitchen paper.

Makes 24 small cakes

3 teaspoons light soft brown sugar
1 tablespoon light soy sauce
350g chicken thighs, boned and skinned
120g toasted peanuts
40g fresh white breadcrumbs
1 tablespoon Thai red curry paste
1 tablespoon lime juice
2 tablespoons chopped coriander
1 tablespoon sweet chilli sauce
vegetable oil for frying

Pork & Cashew Meatballs

These are an unusual canapé – the recipe was given to me by a lovely friend Margaret Andrew with whom I cooked for so many celebrities at the BBC years ago before they cut down on their entertaining. Margaret always says she's not keen on cooking but honestly, she is one of the best chefs/cooks I have ever worked with – her understanding of flavours is just perfect. We served these in many a Green Room after a show. Serve cold with the soy dressing.

Makes 25

For the pork balls
450g pork mince
100g dried peaches or apricots
2 garlic cloves, finely chopped
pinch cayenne pepper
50g unsalted cashew nuts
salt and freshly ground black pepper
oil for frying

For the dressing
15ml light soy sauce
15ml lemon juice
30ml sunflower oil

Soak the dried peaches in the boiling water for 5 minutes and then drain and chop finely.

Add chopped peaches to the pork mince along with the garlic, cayenne pepper, salt and freshly ground black pepper. Mix very well and with wet hands form it into very small balls with a cashew nut in the middle of each ball.

Put the oil into a heavy-based frying pan and when hot fry the balls for 10–15 minutes. Remove them to a plate and leave to cool.

Serve at room temperature with the dressing poured over – all you have to do to make the dressing is mix all the ingredients together.

Prawn & Caramelised Onion Pancakes

These versatile canapé bases I have been making for about 20 years. Lovely, and a change from normal blinis. They freeze beautifully and you can just defrost and put the sour cream and caramelised onion on just before serving. An old-fashioned recipe, but really worth doing.

Makes about 45

Pancakes
500g raw prawns
110g plain flour
1 egg, lightly beaten
180ml buttermilk
40g butter, melted
1 tablespoon chopped fresh tarragon

Topping for pancakes
250ml sour cream or crème fraîche
10g fresh coriander leaves, flat-leaf parsley separated or micro herbs

Caramelised onion (perhaps buy a really good jar from Waitrose/a good deli)
50g butter
300g red Spanish onion, finely sliced
2 tablespoons light soft brown sugar
1 tablespoon balsamic vinegar
¼ teaspoon freshly ground black pepper
60ml water

Melt butter in pan, add onion, cook covered over low heat for 5 minutes.

Add sugar, vinegar, pepper and water, stir over low heat for about 15 minutes or until onion is very soft and mixture is thick and syrupy; cool.

Pancakes

Shell and de-vein prawns, finely chop.

Sift flour into bowl.

Whisk in beaten egg, buttermilk and butter until smooth.

Stir in prawns and tarragon.

Drop rounded teaspoons of mixture in batches, into greased heavy-based pan, cook until bubbles appear. Turn pancakes, cook until browned on both sides. Repeat with remaining mixture.

Spoon sour cream onto pancakes; top with caramelised onion then coriander.

Puff's Cheese Puffs!

This is a simple and delicious canapé recipe given to me by my son's wonderful stepmother, Puff. She asked me to add them to a list of canapés I was doing for a party of hers; initially, looking at the ingredients, I was sceptical. But it really was so good.

Makes 24

6 ordinary white sliced bread stamped out into small rounds
125g cream cheese
125g Hellmann's mayonnaise
150g Parmesan, grated
4 tablespoons finely chopped chives
¼ teaspoon cayenne pepper

Preheat the oven to 180°C.

Mix all the ingredients together and spread onto each round of bread.

Bake in oven for about 10 minutes.

Courgette, Leek & Feta Frittata Canapés

These are very easy to make and also freeze well. You could cut them into larger squares and serve them with a simple watercress salad for a starter. They are rather like a rich quiche mix without the pastry so a good alternative for any coeliac friends you may have.

Makes 50

1 tablespoon light olive oil
20g butter
2 medium courgettes, coarsely grated
2 small leeks, sliced
1 garlic clove, crushed
8 eggs, lightly beaten
125ml single cream
100g feta cheese, crumbled
40g Parmesan, grated
2 tablespoons chopped fresh mint
2 tablespoons polenta
2 tablespoons Parmesan, grated and a bit extra
50g feta cheese, crumbled

Preheat oven to 180°C.

Grease 23cm square slab pan, cover base with foil.

Heat oil and butter in frying pan, add courgette, leeks and garlic. Stir for 3 minutes then cover and cook until leeks are soft; cool.

Combine leek mixture with eggs, cream, cheeses and mint in a bowl; pour into prepared pan.

Sprinkle with combined polenta and extra cheeses.

Bake in oven for about 40 minutes or until set.

Leave to cool in the pan then cut frittata into 25 squares and then cut each square in half diagonally.

Parmesan Biscuits

I had put in two recipes for Parmesan biscuits but thought that was a bit daft, so I have just cooked both of them to put them to the test and this wins by a margin. I used really good cheddar and the smell in the kitchen of lovely cheddar biscuits baking in the oven was just amazing.

Makes about 25 little biscuits

- 100g butter, cubed
- 100g plain flour
- ½ teaspoon sea salt
- ½ teaspoon cayenne pepper
- ½ teaspoon English mustard powder
- 50g mature cheddar, grated
- 50g Parmesan, grated
- 1 egg, beaten

Preheat the oven to 180°C.

Put the butter, flour, salt, cayenne pepper and mustard powder in the liquidiser. Pulse for a minute or two and then add the grated cheeses. Once the mixture clumps together like pastry – tip it out of the liquidiser and place it on a floured surface and bring it all together.

Wrap it in cling film and place in the fridge for an hour.

Take it out of the fridge and put it on a floured work surface and roll it out to 2mm thick.

Get a 3cm biscuit cutter and gently stamp out rounds.

Place rounds on a baking tray lined with non-stick baking paper and bake in the oven for 10 minutes until well browned.

Take them out of the oven and carefully put them on a wire rack to cool.

Liz's Wonderful Croque Monsieurs

These are one of the most popular canapés we do – especially when we serve them late on in the evening when people have had a few drinks. Just use cheap white sliced bread if you like, or sometimes we have used really good, sliced sourdough bread, but both are nice. These are probably not very good for the waistline but worth the extra calories I feel.

Makes 60 little squares

1 sliced white loaf (about 20 slices)
125g butter, melted
small amount of light olive oil
10 slices of cheddar or Gruyère
10 slices of ham
grainy mustard or Dijon mustard

Spread mustard over 10 slices of the bread.

Lay ham then cheese on the mustard and top with the other slices of bread.

Melt some of the butter in a frying pan and put in a teaspoon of light olive oil – this prevents the butter burning. Once the fat is frothing put in the sandwich and brown it on both sides. Repeat with the remaining sandwiches, adding more butter and oil as you see fit. Leave them to cool as you go along spread out on racks – lay some kitchen paper under the racks to catch the drips.

Once completely cool cut the crusts off and cut each sandwich into 6 little squares. Liz uses an electric knife but you could use a really good bread knife.

Tip You can either serve these straight away or once completely cold, freeze them. Then, on the day you want to eat them, just take them out of the freezer, let them defrost a bit and pop them in a very hot oven for about 8 minutes or until piping hot.

Chicken & Walnut Sandwiches

You may find this an odd addition to my book but we cater for so many different events including funerals. Years ago a friend helped me do a large funeral and made these – we have made them ever since. They are such good sandwiches and wonderful for any picnic or teatime treat. You can also leave out the nuts. If you want to make these a few hours in advance of eating them just wrap them very well in cling film or equivalent to stop them from drying out.

Makes 9 whole sandwiches cut into quarters – 36 quarters

18 slices wholegrain bread (really fresh)
120g soft butter
400g cooked chicken, chopped
120g crème fraîche
150g mayonnaise
300g celery stalks, finely chopped
40g chopped walnuts
50g rocket leaves, chopped

Mix the chicken, crème fraîche, mayonnaise, celery, nuts and rocket all together and season.

Butter the bread slices lightly and then sandwich together with the chicken mixture.

Using a sharp serrated knife trim away the crusts and cut the sandwiches into quarters.

Haloumi & Avocado Bruschetta

This is an excellent vegetarian canapé option – you can make the roasted flatbreads in advance and keep them in an airtight container, but the haloumi must be made at the last minute.

Serves 25

Preheat the oven to 180°C.

Line two baking trays with non-stick baking paper.

Cut the flatbreads into 25 rectangles 4x8cm each and paint each side with light olive oil.

Put bread on baking trays and bake in hot oven for 6 minutes, or until lightly browned. Take out and leave to cool on a rack.

Cut haloumi into 25 thin slices and dry on kitchen paper for 5 minutes.

400g flatbreads (if possible from an Iranian supermarket)
2 tablespoons light olive oil
500g haloumi
3 medium avocados, roughly chopped
1 medium red onion, finely chopped
10 on-the-vine cherry tomatoes, finely chopped
1 tablespoon extra-virgin olive oil
1 tablespoon lemon juice
40g baby rocket leaves

Mix avocado, tomato, onion and extra-virgin olive oil together with salt. Pour over the lemon juice.

Fry haloumi in batches in a large frying pan which you have painted with a bit of light olive oil, for 1 minute each side until brown.

Put each piece of haloumi on the flatbread and top with the avocado mixture and a few rocket leaves to serve.

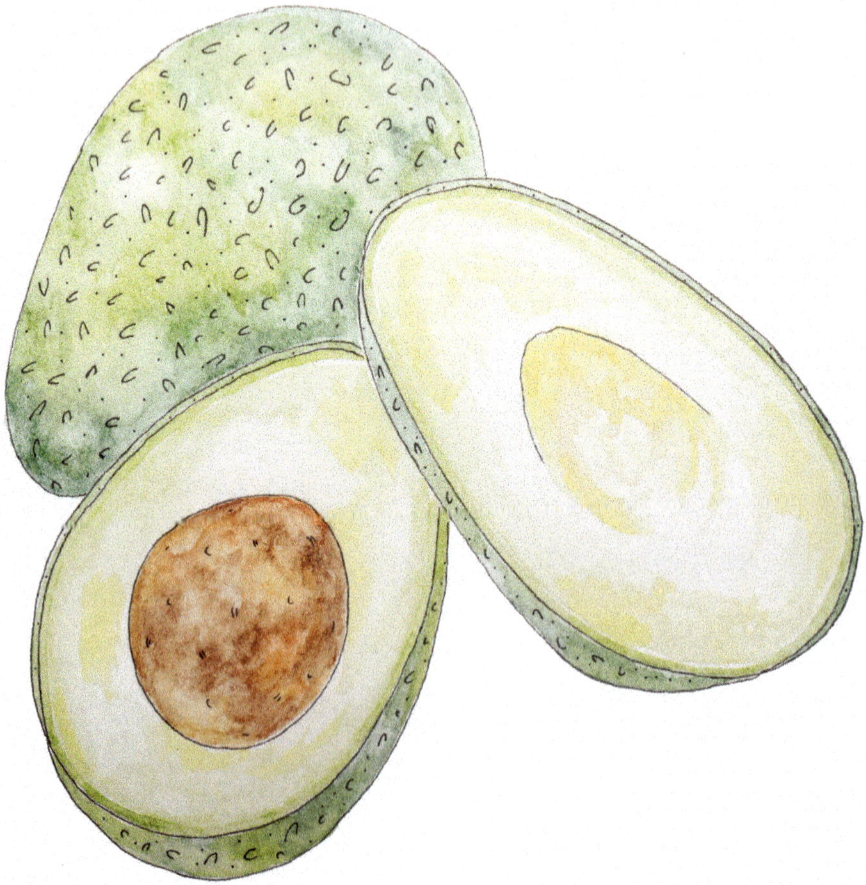

Starters

Chicken Liver Pâté

There are so many different recipes for chicken liver pâté but this one is excellent. My brother Jono loves this type of food and I love cooking for him!

Serves 4

125g chicken livers trimmed
1 small onion, finely chopped
100g butter
1 teaspoon dry sherry or brandy
salt and freshly ground black pepper
225ml water

Put the chicken livers in the salted water and bring to the boil. As soon as it boils, turn off the heat. Cover the pan and leave for 10 minutes.

Melt the butter and gently fry the chopped onion until soft.

Put the liver and onions into a liquidiser with pepper and the sherry or brandy. Once liquidised put into individual serving dishes – a small ramekin or something similar.

Melt a bit more butter and pour on top of each dish to seal the pâté – you could either freeze or keep in the fridge for up to 4 days – it keeps well.

Cucumber & Cream Cheese Mousse

This is another very old-fashioned but excellent recipe which we used to do when I was a chalet girl forty-five years ago. It was popular then and is still popular with my clients now.

Serves 12

2 medium cucumbers
500g cream cheese
300ml mayonnaise
150ml cold water with 2 tablespoons of white wine vinegar in it
1 teaspoon salt
4 teaspoons sugar
30g gelatine
150ml double cream, lightly whipped

Line 12 small ramekins with cling film.

Peel and seed cucumbers. Cut lengthways and finely dice and sprinkle with salt. Leave in colander for 30 minutes – drain and dry with kitchen paper.

Put the water and vinegar in a small heavy saucepan, sprinkle on the gelatine and soak for 5 minutes. Place over low heat and stir until gelatine is dissolved – do not boil. Add salt and sugar.

Stir cooled gelatine into mayonnaise and cream cheese and whip together.

Whip cream lightly and stir into the cream cheese mix. Add chopped cucumber and give a good stir.

Pour into lined ramekins and put in fridge to set.

Turn them out onto your starter plate on a few watercress and rocket leaves and decorate with the cucumber ribbons. Serve with Melba toast.

To make the Melba toast, buy some thick sliced white bread and toast in a toaster. Cool the pieces of toast and then cut off the crusts and cut each piece in two widthways. Preheat the oven to 200°C and place the half-cooked toast pieces in the oven and carefully watch until they are dry and crispy – so easy to burn. The Melba toast will keep in a good airtight container for weeks.

Home-Cured Salmon with Beetroot, Horseradish Cream & Pickled Cucumber

We have done this so many times as a starter at weddings and people love it! It looks lovely with the different colours. If you make it for 16 but only need it for 4 or so, you can freeze it once sliced, lined with greaseproof paper between the slices, and take it out to defrost as and when you need it. It really freezes very well.

Serves 16 (couple of slices per head)

For the salmon
2 skin-on salmon fillets
200g caster sugar
85g fresh horseradish, peeled and finely grated, or grated horseradish from a jar
3 medium raw beetroot, coarsely grated (no need to peel)
140g sea salt
1 small bunch dill, chopped

For the horseradish cream
600ml crème fraîche mixed with 2 tablespoons horseradish

Pickled cucumber
1 medium cucumber, deseeded, peeled and thinly sliced
1 tablespoon white wine vinegar
½ teaspoon sea salt
½ teaspoon caster sugar

Lay the salmon fillets, skin side down, on a board and brush your hand along it. If you feel any little pin bones pinch them out with your fingers or tweezers.

In a bowl, mix all of the other ingredients for the salmon together to make the cure.

Stretch two large sheets of cling film over a work surface and spoon over some of the cure.

Lay one of the fillets skin side down, on the cure, then pack over most of the cure and sandwich with the remaining fillet, skin side up. Top with the last of the cure and wrap both fillets together tightly with lots of cling film, place in a container with sides (like a large roasting tin). Put a smaller tray on top and weigh it down with a few heavy tins or bricks.

Leave in the fridge for at least three days or up to a week. Don't be alarmed by the amount of liquid that leaks out, this is normal. Once a day, pour away the liquid, turn the salmon and re-apply the weights.

To serve

Unwrap the salmon from the cling film and brush off the marinade.

Slice the salmon into thin slivers. Add a handful of salad and drizzle with the dressing. Once made, the salmon will sit happily in the fridge for up to a week and can be used just like smoked salmon.

Serve with horseradish cream. Just mix the crème fraîche with the horseradish and some pickled cucumber. To pickle cucumber, just mix the cucumber with the vinegar, salt and sugar.

Double-Baked Cheese Soufflés

Again, an old-fashioned recipe but I love it. It makes a wonderful starter or a simple supper on its own with a bag of watercress, spinach and rocket salad tossed in balsamic dressing and some lovely sourdough bread. Don't be put off by thinking this is difficult to make, or worry about serving it before it collapses – these twice baked ones don't collapse the second time around in baking – they are more solid and easy to deal with.

Preheat the oven to 200°C.

Generously butter 6 x 150ml ovenproof ramekins and line the bases with a disc of baking parchment. Place in a deep baking tray.

Put the onion in the saucepan with the milk and bay leaf, bring to simmer and cook for five minutes. Don't let it boil. Remove from heat and let cool for a few minutes.

Melt the butter in a pan and add the flour. Strain the milk into the flour mixture and bring to the boil, stirring constantly. Add the cheddar, mustard and nutmeg and stir until the cheese melts.

Test the seasoning and transfer the sauce to a bowl to cool. Beat in the egg yolks.

Serves 6

1 small onion, peeled and sliced
275ml full-fat milk
1 bay leaf
40g butter, plus extra for greasing
40g plain flour
100g cheddar, grated
1 teaspoon English mustard or 2 teaspoons Dijon mustard
freshly grated nutmeg to taste
salt and freshly ground black pepper
4 eggs, separated

For the second baking

50g Gruyère or mature cheddar, grated
6 tablespoons single cream

Whisk the egg whites until stiff, fold into the cheese mixture.

Spoon the mixture into the ramekins to the top.

Fill the baking tray with boiling water, halfway up the sides of the ramekins and bake in the centre of the oven for 20 minutes. Once cooked, remove from the oven and leave the soufflés to cool in the ramekins.

When cold, line a baking tray with baking parchment and slide a knife around the edge of each ramekin. Place on the baking sheet upside down.

At this stage you could freeze the soufflés or just use straight away. 15 minutes before serving, sprinkle with the grated Gruyère or cheddar and spoon a tablespoon of cream over each soufflé. Bake for ten minutes and serve quickly with the salad.

Gazpacho

This doesn't sound as if it will be tasty but the knack is to get the best tomato juice you can buy – it has to be fresh and squeezed from tomatoes, not from concentrate. This is another recipe from the cookery school I went to years ago – it really is good. So many people have questioned me and doubted that one should really be using fresh tomatoes until they try this recipe and now swear by it!

Liquidise the tomato juice and all the vegetables and add the lemon juice and oils. Add the salt, cayenne pepper and Tabasco.

Chill until you want to eat it – you could decorate it with small croutons or finely chopped cucumber or peppers.

Serves 6

1 litre fresh tomato juice (I get mine from Waitrose)
1 small red pepper, deseeded and finely chopped
½ small green pepper, deseeded and finely chopped
½ small red onion, finely chopped
3 garlic cloves, peeled and chopped
1 cucumber, peeled, deseeded and finely chopped
2 shakes of Tabasco
8 tablespoons lemon juice
6 tablespoons light olive oil
6 tablespoons extra-virgin olive oil
salt
cayenne pepper

Goat's Cheese & Red Pepper Pâté

This is the most lovely dip or pâté to serve with soda bread, toast or crudités as a starter or before-dinner snack. Sophie Stork gave me the recipe and it always reminds me of happy weekends at her beautiful house in East Sussex. It would also be very good on a picnic with lots of lovely bits and bobs to dip into it.

Serves 6–8

2 large red peppers
1 tablespoon light olive oil
300g full-fat cream cheese
200g soft goat's cheese
2 tablespoons runny honey
1 small bunch chives
salt and freshly ground black pepper

Preheat the oven to 200°C.

Place the red peppers on an oven tray lined with Bakewell paper. Bake for 30 minutes and then leave to cool. Once cool deseed and skin.

Place the cream cheese, goat's cheese and honey into a food processor and pulse to mix well. Add the chives and pulse again, season with salt and pepper and give it one last pulse.

Slice the peppers.

Place the cream cheese mixture into a serving dish – lay the peppers on top and then put the remaining cheese mixture on top and spread flat. Chill well for at least a couple of hours and then serve with soda bread, toast or crudités.

Mushroom Pâté

I have had this recipe for about 30 years – it is such a good alternative for vegetarians if you are serving something like Chicken Liver Pâté. So easy as well. Years ago my brother had a nanny to help with his son Alexander and she made this for him – he loved it and so did I!

Fry the mushrooms in the butter until soft and then blend all the ingredients in a food processor. Put into a nice serving bowl and cool until set.

Serve it from the bowl at the table with some hot toast to spread it on.

Serves 6

250g chestnut mushrooms
60g butter
30g breadcrumbs
2 onions, finely sliced
125g cream or curd cheese
freshly grated nutmeg
salt and freshly ground black pepper
1 teaspoon lemon juice

Parma Ham & Rocket Wraps

This looks very impressive and is easy to make – especially if you are neat with your hands. My cook Liz makes these beautifully as she has great patience. They are light and a delicious starter at any dinner party.

Serves 6

- 12 fine green beans, topped and tailed
- 120g rocket
- 100g pine nuts, roasted
- 2 tablespoons freshly grated Parmesan
- 20ml extra-virgin olive oil
- juice of 1 lemon
- 12 slices Parma ham or prosciutto

Dressing

- 20ml balsamic vinegar
- 60ml extra-virgin olive oil
- salt and freshly ground black pepper
- 1 tablespoon chopped flat-leaf parsley

Put the beans into a bowl and pour boiling water over to cover – leave for 1 minute and then drain and refresh under very cold water until the beans are ice cold. Dry the beans.

Mix the beans with the rocket leaves, pine nuts and Parmesan and drizzle with the olive oil and lemon juice. Season with salt and pepper to taste.

Lay out the Parma ham slices and put a handful of the bean and rocket mixture on each. Roll them up nicely and then drizzle with the dressing. All you have to do with that is whisk the ingredients together in a bowl.

Cream of Pea & Mint Soup

This is a divine simple soup recipe which is hugely easy to make and most people would always have these ingredients in the freezer. If you don't have any fresh mint you could always use dried mint, which is an excellent alternative. It is very important not to cook the peas for more than a couple of minutes so you keep the lovely green colour.

Melt butter in a pan and soften onion for 10 minutes. Then add chopped potato with the hot stock or water and simmer for 20 minutes.

Add peas and simmer for 2 minutes.

Put the soup with the mint in a food processor and pulse until smooth. Add the cream.

If too thick add some hot water and then salt and freshly ground black pepper to taste.

Serves 4

60g butter
1 onion, chopped
1 medium potato, chopped
1 litre hot chicken stock or water
350g frozen peas
1 handful fresh mint, chopped
125ml milk or cream
salt and freshly ground black pepper

Potted Shrimps

I just love this – albeit expensive and quite a lot of butter – but gosh it is worth it as a treat sometimes. A lovely simple starter or a snacky lunch... or simple at-home supper. Wiz Deakin my friend loves them! You can buy delicious ready-made ones from a good fishmonger but we make our own here.

Serves 6

175g good butter
pinch cayenne pepper
pinch mace
¼ teaspoon freshly grated nutmeg
800ml fresh shrimps
salt and freshly ground black pepper
juice of 1 lemon

To clarify the butter, very gently melt it over a low heat, skimming any foam off the top but not stirring. When the butter is melted, remove from the heat and leave to stand for 1 minute, so that the milk solids settle to the bottom. Carefully pour off the golden clarified butter into a jug and discard the solids left in the pan. Allow to cool before using.

Divide the butter, putting one half into a small bowl and add the pinch of cayenne pepper, the pinch of mace and the freshly grated nutmeg. Add the salt and freshly ground black pepper and the lemon juice. Taste before adding the shrimps.

Divide the shrimp mixture between 6 little dishes – small ramekins are perfect. Put the ramekins into the fridge to set. When set put the remaining clarified butter on top of each dish and put them back into the fridge to set again.

Remember to take them out of the fridge 15 minutes before you want to eat them. Delicious served with homemade Melba toast.

Really Good Cucumber & Yoghurt Soup for Summer

Again, we have served this at many a wedding. It is different and makes a lovely light summer starter – so easy to put together as well. You can decorate the soup with chopped dill and a shaving of cucumber, which looks great. Jenny Brown, a delightful Australian foody friend of mine, gave me this recipe.

Serves 8

Place the cucumber, walnuts, garlic, spring onions, mint, dill and tarragon leaves in the food processor and pulse. Add the chilli, stock, yoghurt, olive oil, lemon juice and cider vinegar. Season with salt and pepper.

Chill and serve in nice bowls decorated with dill and cucumber shavings and drizzle with some extra-virgin olive oil.

1 large cucumber, peeled, deseeded and chopped (keep a bit for decoration)
100g chopped walnuts
2 garlic cloves, chopped
4 white and green spring onions, chopped
1 small bunch mint
1 small bunch dill (keep a bit for decoration)
1 small bunch tarragon
½ teaspoon dried red chilli
250ml homemade chicken stock
200g full-fat yoghurt
150ml light olive oil
juice of 1 lemon
2 tablespoons really good cider vinegar
salt and freshly ground black pepper
extra-virgin olive oil for decoration

Shona's Sun-Dried Tomatoes with Red Peppers & Olives – Mixture for Canapés

This is a delicious mixture which you could put on a bruschetta for a starter. I have no idea where I got it from but have been serving it for years either as a starter or on small bruschettas as a canapé.

Makes enough for 20 little canapé toppings

3 medium red peppers
1 tablespoon light olive oil
1 small red Spanish onion, finely chopped
2 tablespoons pine nuts, toasted
40g canned black olives, pitted
40g sun-dried tomatoes in oil, drained and chopped
2 tablespoons fresh basil, chopped
Parmesan

Quarter peppers, remove seeds and membranes.

Grill peppers or bake in a hot oven, skin side up until skin blisters and blackens. Peel away skin, finely chop peppers.

Heat oil in pan, add onion and fry until soft. Then add nuts, olives and tomatoes. Add peppers and basil, cook 2 minutes.

Put a teaspoon onto a small bruschetta and serve with a shaving of Parmesan.

This can be made in advance and it also freezes well.

Sea Bass Ceviche with Avocado & Red Chilli

This is such a delicious and simple starter. Do use really good sea bass from a fishmonger – Michael's Fish Shop in Barnes, London is the best. I urge people who think they don't like raw fish to try this – it is absolutely wonderful. I have tried to copy a ceviche I had almost every day for lunch in Lamu, Kenya. I think I have got it right – it is very easy.

Cut slices from the skinned sea bass fillet and put them in a shallow dish with the red onion, red chilli and pour over the lime juice, salt and freshly ground black pepper. It only takes about 5 minutes to cure.

Slice the avocado and add to the sea bass – top with the chilli and the chopped coriander.

Serves 4

400g sea bass fillets, skinned
½ small red onion, peeled and finely sliced
1 red chilli, deseeded and finely sliced
juice of 2 limes
salt and freshly ground black pepper
2 avocados
1 small bunch coriander, roughly chopped

Starters

Shona's Fresh Salmon Starter with Sweet & Salted Cucumber with Dill

Another lovely raw fresh fish starter which is so popular at the moment. This is very easy to do and can be made and kept in the fridge for a couple of hours until you need to serve it. Again, please buy your salmon from a good fishmonger for this.

Serves 4

Salmon mixture
200g fresh salmon fillet, skinned
1 tablespoon capers, rinsed, drained and chopped
2 spring onions, finely chopped
juice of 2 lemons
2 tablespoons light olive oil
freshly ground black pepper
salt to taste

Cucumber mixture
1 cucumber, peeled, deseeded and finely chopped
1 tablespoon dill, finely chopped
1 tablespoon white wine vinegar
1 teaspoon caster sugar
1 teaspoon sea salt

To make the cucumber – put the cubed cucumber, dill, white wine vinegar, caster sugar and salt into a bowl and leave to infuse.

To make the salmon – cube the salmon into tiny dice and put in a bowl with the capers, spring onions, lemon juice, oil and pepper. Taste to see if the mixture needs any more salt and then put covered in the fridge until you want to eat.

Shona's Popular Summer Wedding Starter

This is great when nectarines are around and lovely and ripe. It's also so simple – anyone can do it as a starter in summer but don't attempt it with nectarines not in season as it will not taste the same. And do buy the best tomatoes you can find. White balsamic vinegar is an alternative to really good cider vinegar. I try and find good mozzarella but, if you can't, the best economical ones I have found are the Tesco or M&S ones – left out at room temperature and served with delicious things, they really are quite good.

Take the stones out of the nectarines and cut into thick slices. Quarter the tomatoes and slice or tear the mozzarella.

Plate the fruit, tomatoes, mozzarella onto lovely plain white starter plates (if you have them) and then sprinkle on the basil, rocket leaves or pea shoots followed by the vinegar, olive oil, salt and freshly ground black pepper. Serve with some yummy crusty bread.

Serves 6

3 large nectarines
200g on-the-vine cherry tomatoes
100g yellow cherry tomatoes
250g good mozzarella
1 bunch basil leaves
handful pea shoots or rocket leaves
salt and freshly ground black pepper
1 tablespoon good cider vinegar
3 tablespoons extra-virgin olive oil

Smoked Salmon & Horseradish Creams

We used to do these when we were chalet girls – not sure where we got the smoked salmon from – maybe guests brought it out to us, but I remember a guest giving us the recipe. They only take a few minutes to make but must be made at least a couple of hours ahead of time to allow the gelatine to set. Serve with brown bread and butter. Serve on a bed of watercress and some finely diced skinned cucumber to decorate, or just with a lovely sprig of dill.

Serves 6

200g smoked salmon
2 teaspoons creamed horseradish
1 sachet gelatine
juice of 2 lemons, made up to ¼ pint with cold water if necessary
300ml double cream
lots of freshly ground black pepper

Line 6 ramekins with cling film.

Put the smoked salmon and horseradish into a liquidiser and blend.

Sprinkle the gelatine onto the lemon juice/water mixture in a small saucepan and heat gently until the granules of the gelatine have completely dissolved.

Add the gelatine mixture to the liquidised mixture and blend to a smooth paste.

Pour in the double cream and season with pepper. Blend thoroughly.

Pour into the 6 ramekins and leave to set.

To turn these out, sit the ramekins in hot water for a few seconds, invert and shake onto your starter plate.

Smoked Trout Pâté / Mousse

A lovely pâté/mousse for a starter. I would serve it with Melba toast and some pickled cucumber – which is cucumber sliced thinly with a teaspoon of white wine vinegar, a teaspoon of caster sugar, a good pinch of salt and some finely chopped fresh dill. It is particularly wonderful if you happen to be in Scotland and can buy really good smoked trout fresh from the Smokery. There is a wonderful one near Dunbar in the Borders in Scotland, which my lovely friend Robin Mitchell introduced me to.

Line 4 ramekins with cling film.

Place all the ingredients into a food processor and whiz until smooth.

Divide the mousse between the ramekins.

Leave them in the fridge until you are ready to eat. Then turn the mousses out and serve with thin brown bread or Melba toast.

Serves 4

125g smoked trout
100g crème fraîche or soft cream cheese
2 teaspoons horseradish cream
juice ½ lemon

Softened Red Onions with Parma Ham, Rocket & Shaved Parmesan

Gosh I love this starter – it is so, so good. Leave out the ham if you want to do it for vegetarians. You could prepare the onions the day before you need to serve it and then just put everything else together at the last minute. The sweetness of the onions goes so well with the salty Parma ham and lovely balsamic dressing topped with the Parmesan and peppery rocket leaves. I'd like to thank Annie Proffit, an old friend of my husband's, for this recipe which she gave me about 25 years ago.

Serves 4

- 350g red onions, finely sliced
- 200g Parma ham
- 110g Parmesan
- 55ml light olive oil
- 1 teaspoon light soft brown sugar
- 1 small bunch fresh thyme leaves
- 2 tablespoons water
- 55ml good balsamic vinegar
- salt and freshly ground black pepper
- 1 bag of rocket (from any supermarket)

Gently fry the sliced onions in the olive oil for about 10 minutes until they are soft. Add the brown sugar, thyme leaves, salt and freshly ground black pepper and 2 tablespoons water.

Cover the pan and cook slowly over a very low heat for about 20 minutes, stirring occasionally. Once the liquid has reduced and caramelised add the balsamic vinegar and leave the mixture to cool.

Arrange the rocket on serving plates and put the onion mixture on top, followed by a layer of ham and then the shaved Parmesan.

Tomato Soup

This is such an easy, delicious and old-fashioned tomato soup recipe that works so well. My brother's first wife, Nicky (always a sister-in-law to me), used to make this when she was a chalet girl and she gave me the recipe (I think). She is the most wonderful cook so probably won't be best pleased when I say that, whenever I make this most simple of soups, I think of her. It reminds me that simple recipes are often the best – a lovely soup to have in the winter with some crusty bread.

Chop the tomatoes roughly and put in a pan with the onion, stock, red wine, vinegar, sugar and salt and freshly ground black pepper. Simmer for 20 minutes.

Blend mixture in liquidiser and then add the cream.

Serves 4–6

750g good tasty tomatoes
1 medium onion, peeled and finely chopped
600ml chicken stock
150ml red wine
15ml red wine vinegar
15ml sugar
salt and freshly ground black pepper
200ml double cream

Crab, Dill, Chives, Cucumber & Avocado Salad / Starter

A lovely way of serving crab as a starter. Do bear in mind that crab is very rich – especially the brown meat – so you do not need masses per person. For 4 people you really only need 375g cooked crab meat. I buy mine from the Barnes Fish Shop – all picked beautifully. We did this at a wedding last year and, though not a cheap starter, it was very popular.

Serves 4

375g cooked crab meat
1 medium cucumber, peeled, deseeded and cut into chunks
1 avocado, peeled and cut into slices
2 limes, cut in half
1 tablespoon finely chopped chives
1 tablespoon finely chopped dill
1 tablespoon finely chopped flat-leaf parsley
1 bag watercress, spinach and rocket

Dressing
1 tablespoon Hellmann's mayonnaise
1 teaspoon seeded mustard
1 tablespoon lemon juice
4 tablespoons extra-virgin olive oil
3 tablespoons of the cooked crab meat – use the brown meat
dash of Tabasco or pinch of cayenne pepper
salt to taste

Make the dressing first – just mix the mayonnaise with the mustard, lemon juice, olive oil, Tabasco or cayenne pepper and salt in a bowl. Sieve the brown crab meat into the sauce. Check seasoning before serving.

Put the white crab meat on to a plate with the watercress, spinach and rocket – add the slices of avocado, the chunks of cucumber, the chopped herbs and pour over the dressing. Serve with the lime halves for each person to squeeze.

Roasted Mediterranean Vegetables with Herb-Baked Ricotta

You need to buy good ricotta from a cheese shop or cheese counter – not the stuff in little plastic pots. Barnes Cheese Shop sells it and I know there are lots of other good cheese shops all over the country. It is a wonderful vegetarian starter to serve at a special dinner; we have done it at a few weddings.

Preheat the oven to 180°C.

Put the aubergines, courgettes, red peppers and onions in a large bowl and toss well with two tablespoons of light olive oil and add salt.

Spread the mixture on a large baking tray lined with non-stick paper, and put in the preheated oven for 45–50 minutes until browned and tender – you will have to do quite a bit of oven checking here.

Place the tomato halves on another oven tray, lined with paper and roast in same oven but only for 15 minutes – drizzle the tomatoes with a bit of light olive oil before roasting.

Serves 6

Vegetables
180g aubergines, halved and sliced into chunks
270g courgettes, sliced into chunks
2 red peppers, deseeded and cut into chunks
200g red onions, peeled and quartered
180g cherry tomatoes, halved
6 large garlic cloves, unpeeled
2 tablespoons light olive oil
4 tablespoons extra-virgin olive oil
fresh oregano leaves or basil to finish off

Ricotta
750g fresh ricotta
1 tablespoon light olive oil

Put the roasted vegetables onto your serving dish and drizzle the extra-virgin olive oil on top.

Place the ricotta on one of the already used baking trays and drizzle with the light olive oil. Bake in the oven for 15 minutes until brown and warmed through.

Put the ricotta on the plate with the vegetables and sprinkle on oregano; if you cannot find fresh oregano, basil will do!

Celeriac Remoulade with Serrano or Parma Ham

I had to include this dish as I love it – I even like the little plastic containers of celeriac remoulade you can buy ready-made in French supermarkets. I just love a French supermarket – I have no idea why I so much prefer them to the big supermarkets here in the UK these days. I drive my husband mad on the way out skiing every year buying all sorts of things which remind me of my happy days spent living in France, working as a chalet girl and on various other jobs all those years ago.

Peel and cut the celeriac into big chunks and then put through the food processor grater. Once grated mix the celeriac with the juice of the lemon.

Leave the celeriac and lemon juice for about 20 minutes until the celeriac softens – the lemon juice will keep the colour. Then mix it with the Dijon mustard, mayonnaise, crème fraîche, salt and freshly ground white pepper.

Serve it with the Parma ham and parsley to decorate.

Serves 4

1 medium celeriac
juice of 1 lemon
pinch of salt and freshly ground white pepper
3 tablespoons homemade mayonnaise or Hellmann's would be OK
2 teaspoons Dijon mustard
1 tablespoon crème fraîche or double cream
1 rounded tablespoon coarsely chopped flat-leaf parsley
8 slices of good Parma ham or Serrano ham to serve

Melting Mozzarella with Toasted Ciabatta Sticks

This is a pleasingly unusual starter which is easy to make, and you can have it all ready and just pop in the oven 15 minutes before you sit down. If you are on a budget, as the mozzarella is going to be cooked, you could use a good supermarket one for something like this. It is basically a yummy thick homemade tomato sauce with some lovely mozzarella melted in. You could also have it as a main course with some pasta.

Serves 8

1 tablespoon light olive oil
1 medium onion
2 garlic cloves, crushed
1 carrot, finely chopped
1 celery stick, finely chopped
1 teaspoon sugar
3 x 400g tin of tomatoes
1 tablespoon tomato purée
salt and freshly ground black pepper
4 x 200g ball of mozzarella, cut in half
1 ciabatta, cut into long sticks and grilled
8 ovenproof ramekins

Preheat the oven to 180°C.

Make the tomato sauce by frying the onion gently for 10 minutes before adding the carrot and celery and frying for another few minutes.

Add the chopped garlic and give a good stir before adding the tinned tomatoes, tomato purée, salt, sugar and pepper. Bubble this gently on a low heat/flame for about 40 minutes then pour into the ramekins.

Put a piece of mozzarella into the centre of each ramekin of sauce and then put the ramekins on a baking tray and place in the centre of oven for about 15 minutes until the cheese is melted.

Serve with toasted/grilled ciabatta.

My Puy Lentil & Kale Soup

I often do a batch of this and freeze it for future suppers – it is so good with lots of grated Parmesan and a hunk of lovely bread. You could use red lentils instead if you don't have Puy lentils in your cupboard. I have also substituted the lentils for any small-shaped pasta – orzo would be a good one. This is more of a main course soup than a starter. My husband, who claims to hate kale or cavolo nero or anything similar, laps it up, completely unaware of what he is eating!

Serves 8

30g butter
3 tablespoons light olive oil
3 medium onions, chopped
3 garlic cloves, peeled and finely chopped
2 medium carrots, peeled and finely chopped
2 large celery sticks, finely chopped
100g chopped pancetta
4 sprigs thyme
2 bay leaves
400g Puy lentils
2 x 400g tin of tomatoes
1 tablespoon tomato purée
2 litres good chicken stock (or water if you don't have any stock)
12 large kale leaves or cavolo nero, stems removed and sliced
salt and freshly ground black pepper
6 tablespoons grated Parmesan

Melt the butter and oil in large heavy pan and gently fry the onions and pancetta for 10 minutes until very soft. Add the garlic, carrots and celery and fry for a few more minutes.

Stir in the Puy lentils, tinned tomatoes, chicken stock, tomato purée, thyme and bay and bubble for 40 minutes until the lentils are soft and the stock is reduced to a lovely soup.

Stir in the kale 5 minutes before serving and add the grated Parmesan before eating.

Salmon Rillettes with Bagel Toasts

Another wonderful recipe – so delicious to have as a starter at a special dinner and the bagel toasts are particularly good with it. This would also be a delicious light lunch with a lovely mixed leaf salad.

Serves 10 in small ramekins

450g skinless salmon fillet
a few peppercorns
1 onion
bay leaf
1 tablespoon sea salt
125g butter, softened
6 shallots, very finely chopped
20ml crème fraîche
250g smoked trout fillets
40ml lemon juice
20ml extra-virgin olive oil
2 egg yolks
1 heaped tablespoon chopped dill, plus a sprig to garnish
clarified butter to top (see page 30)

For the bagel toasts
2 large bagels or 4 mini bagels
olive oil, to brush

Preheat the oven to 180°C.

I cook my salmon fillet in a fish kettle – I cover it with water, a few peppercorns, an onion and bay leaf, then bring the fish kettle to the boil and turn it off when it reaches boiling point and leave to cool in the liquid. Or you could bake it on a piece of non-stick paper on a baking tray in oven for about 20 minutes until it is cooked. I prefer the fish kettle way.

Melt 40g of butter in a frying pan over medium heat. Add the shallots and cook, stirring for 10 minutes or until soft. Add a pinch of salt.

Put the remaining 85g of butter in a bowl and use an electric whisk to beat until pale. Add the crème fraîche and beat in well.

Break the steamed salmon and smoked trout into pieces and add to the bowl with the shallots, lemon juice, oil, egg yolks and dill. Beat gently until the mixture is combined but still coarse – season well.

Place in the ramekins and cover with a centimetre layer of cooled clarified butter.

Top with the dill sprig, then cover with plastic wrap and chill for at least 1 hour. The rillettes will keep for three days in the fridge.

For the bagels

Cut the bagels or mini bagels into two half rings, then slice thinly. Spread in a single layer on a baking tray, brush with olive oil and rub with the cut side of garlic clove. Bake for 2–3 minutes until golden, then leave to cool. The bagel toasts will keep in an airtight container for three days.

Fennel & Mozzarella Salad

This sounds like an unusual mixture but it works very well. A friend served it up at a dinner party a few years ago and I wrote down the ingredients and have successfully made it many times since. You do need some really good bread to mop this up with.

Serves 4

3 fennel bulbs, trimmed and sliced so they are really thin
2 large balls mozzarella, torn into bits
juice of 2 lemons
125ml extra-virgin olive oil
salt

Place the mozzarella in the bottom of an attractive serving dish and cover with the thin slices of fennel.

Pour over the lemon juice and olive oil and sea salt.

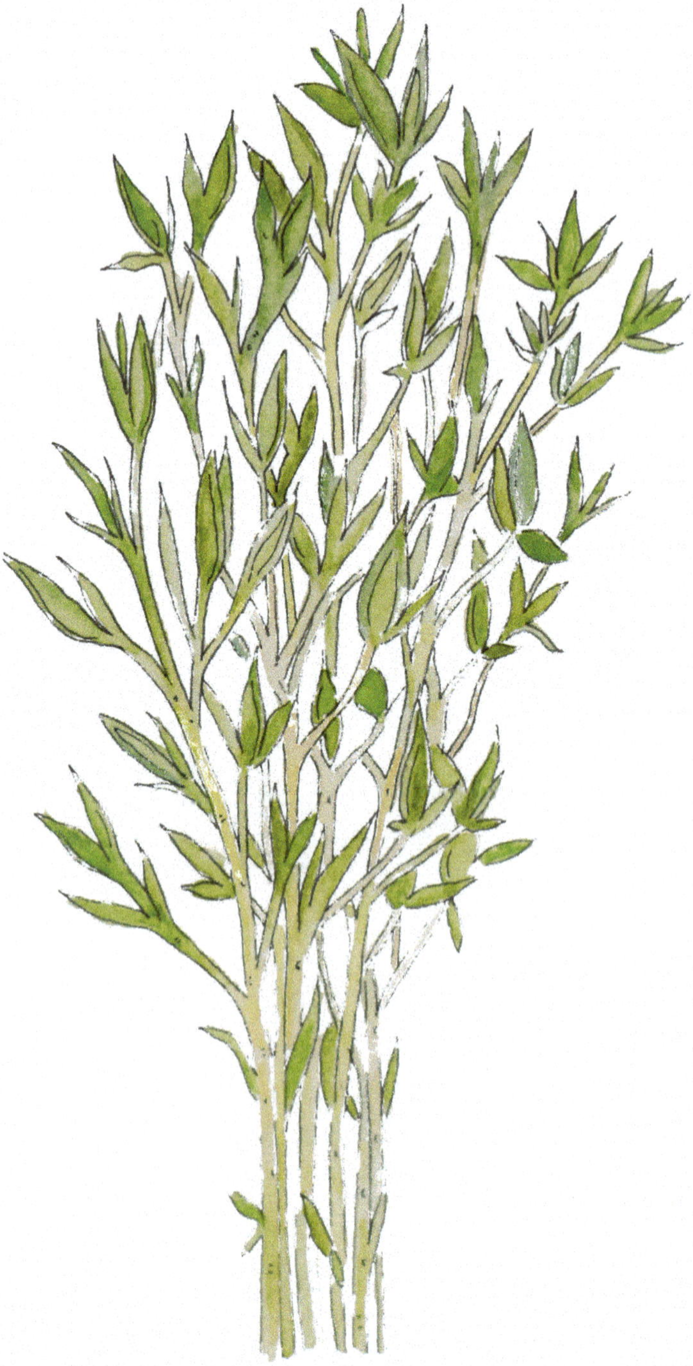

Sides & Salads

Briam

I make this dish whenever I have surplus vegetables in my cupboard/ fridge – aubergines, courgettes, red onions, potatoes or sweet potatoes, peppers and tomatoes. It is such a simple dish to make and really a simple version of the good old French Ratatouille. I usually make it in an old Le Creuset dish my friends, Kip Fyler and Georgie Fry, gave me for a wedding present and I always think of them when I get the dish out!

Serves 6–8

450g red onions, finely sliced
450g aubergines, sliced
450g courgettes, sliced
450g sweet potatoes, peeled and cut into chunks
2 x 400g cans of good plum tomatoes
250g red or yellow peppers, deseeded and sliced
4 garlic cloves, peeled and thinly sliced
250ml light olive oil
250ml water
salt and freshly ground black pepper

Preheat the oven to 170°C.

Spoon some olive oil into the bottom of the oven dish and then literally layer the vegetables up in the pan – alternating them as you go with a tablespoon of tomatoes on top of each layer. Within each layer add thin slices of garlic, a little oil and a sprinkling of salt and freshly ground black pepper. When complete, pour on the water and any remaining olive oil.

Put a lid on the casserole and put it in the oven and cook for an hour and a half – test again for seasoning and serve either on its own as a vegetarian meal or as a side dish to slow-cooked shoulder of lamb or simple roast chicken.

Tip I often make a huge vat of this and freeze it in little containers – you can take one out whenever you feel like a light lunch or supper and either microwave or heat gently on top of the stove.

Bulgur Wheat with Pomegranates

You could also make this with quinoa if you want to be gluten-free but I think it is much nicer with bulgur. It is very good served with a tagine, a chicken dish with sauce or just on its own with lots of roasted vegetables. We serve this with lots of different dishes at weddings – it goes particularly well with chicken in yoghurt and spices, but also with salmon or even slow-cooked lamb.

Halve the pomegranates and, holding them over a bowl, beat the fruit with a wooden spoon. The seeds should just spill out. Remove any coarse bits of white membrane still attached.

Make the dressing by whisking all the dressing ingredients together and season with salt and pepper.

Cook the bulgur wheat in a large pan of boiling water for 10 minutes and then drain thoroughly. When cool add the dressing, and just before you eat, add the parsley, mint, coriander, pomegranate seeds and pistachios.

Serves 6

200g coarse bulgur wheat or quinoa
55g shelled pistachio nuts
1 pomegranate, deseeded
40g flat-leaf parsley, roughly chopped
20g fresh coriander, roughly chopped
10g fresh mint, roughly chopped

Dressing
juice of 2 limes
½ teaspoon maple syrup
½ teaspoon harissa paste
2 tablespoons light olive oil
2 tablespoons extra-virgin olive oil
salt and freshly ground black pepper

Caponata

This is lovely served as a dip with toasted sourdough bread or even as a starter or as an accompaniment to some grilled chicken or meat. Again, it is like ratatouille but with more of a tang from the capers and olives. It freezes well. A lovely young chef, Ali Pumphrey, who used to work for me gave me this recipe.

Serves 6

3 large aubergines, chopped into small chunks
2 tablespoons light olive oil
2 celery sticks, chopped finely
2 small red onions, chopped
2 teaspoons light soft brown sugar
2 garlic cloves, chopped
400g tin cherry tomatoes
4 tablespoons wine vinegar
75g capers
75g green olives, stoned
15g flat-leaf parsley

Preheat the oven to 200°C.

Toss aubergines in the light olive oil and salt – bake in a hot oven for about 30 minutes until brown.

Fry onions gently in some of the light olive oil until soft and then add the celery.

Add the garlic and then the tin of tomatoes plus the sugar and season to taste.

Simmer for about 20 minutes before adding the vinegar and capers and then bubble for another 30 minutes.

Add the green olives and flat-leaf parsley.

Carrots Vichy

My absolute favourite way of doing carrots. So good to do with a roast as you can shove them in the oven and forget about them – obviously a separate oven from the one you are roasting your meat in. Use nice big older carrots, sliced fairly chunkily.

Preheat the oven to 140°C.

Wrap the ingredients in a large sheet of tin foil and cook in the oven for 2 hours.

Serves 6

1kg carrots, peeled and sliced thickly
2 teaspoons sugar
1 teaspoon ground rock salt
50g butter

Cheat's Caesar Salad

I used to go to all the trouble of making a Caesar salad from scratch with homemade mayonnaise, but once I found this recipe using good old Hellmann's I have never looked back. You could always add cooked chicken to this and some sliced avocado. We do this with the lettuce chopped very finely as a canapé, either served in a spoon or on a little bit of baked and oiled bread.

Serves 4

1 small cos lettuce
2 little gem lettuces
1 handful of rocket leaves
shavings of Parmesan

Croutons
50g crustless white bread, cut into cubes
1 tablespoon light olive oil
1 garlic clove
1 tablespoon finely grated Parmesan

Dressing
2 tablespoons mayonnaise
dash of Lea & Perrins Worcestershire sauce
juice ½ lemon
1 tablespoon grated Parmesan

Preheat the oven to 180°C.

Make the croutons. Place the cubes of bread in a bowl together with 1 tablespoon olive oil and 1 tablespoon Parmesan plus the crushed garlic clove. Stir and toss to cover the bread in the oil and cheese and bake on a baking sheet for 10 minutes until crisp and brown.

Make the dressing by mixing all the dressing ingredients together in a bowl.

Break up the lettuce leaves and toss together with dressing in a bowl.

Put the croutons on top with the Parmesan shavings.

Dauphinoise

There are so many good recipes for dauphinoise but these two are my favourites – both from the cookery school I attended in the 1970s in London. Don't use semi-skimmed milk or skimmed milk – it can lead to the mixture separating when cooking.

Serves 4–6

750g waxy potatoes, peeled and thinly sliced
250ml double cream
100ml whole milk
2 small garlic cloves, crushed
½ teaspoon freshly grated nutmeg
50g grated Gruyère

Preheat the oven to 160°C.

Butter a gratin dish.

Put the cream and milk together in a large non-stick pan and add the potatoes – season well and add the garlic and nutmeg. Bring the pan to the boil and then turn the heat right down and simmer for 10 minutes until the potatoes are softened but not cooked all the way through. Keep the heat very slow to avoid burning the milk/cream at the bottom of the pan.

Spoon the potatoes into the buttered dish and cover with the milk and double cream – cover with foil and bake for 30 minutes.

Take off the foil and add the grated cheese and cook for a further 10 minutes until bubbling.

Tip You can make this in advance and cook completely – cool and then warm up in oven for about 20 minutes – covered with tin foil.

Mrs Russell's Favourite Gratin Dauphinoise

A deliciously rich gratin recipe from my cooking school. This is probably easier than the one above and slightly richer, as there is more double cream and no milk.

Serves 6

1kg waxy potatoes
300ml double cream
8 tablespoons grated Gruyère
4 tablespoons grated Parmesan
50g butter
salt and freshly ground black pepper
1 garlic clove, crushed

Preheat the oven to 180°C.

Mix garlic with half the melted butter and rub over the base of a good gratin dish.

Peel and slice the potatoes thinly and line the dish with one layer of potatoes. Sprinkle with a tablespoon double cream, cheese and season with salt and pepper. Repeat until the gratin dish is full – topping with cheese and the rest of the butter. Cook in oven for 1½ hours. If it gets too brown cover with foil.

Potatoes with Lemon & Thyme

These are completely delicious and great with fish, roast lamb or rack of lamb or any simple type of chicken. I have been doing deliveries to my clients during the Covid lockdown and this has proved very popular served with roast cod or monkfish.

Serves 4

Preheat the oven to 180°C.

Cut potatoes into 6 lengthways.

Put potatoes into a large roasting tin and pour over the olive oil, butter, water, lemon zest and juice and mix together until the potatoes are well coated.

Roast for 45 minutes, turning them every 15 minutes.

750g large potatoes
juice of 2 lemons
4 tablespoons light olive oil
1 tablespoon water
zest of 1 lemon
60g butter, diced
2 tablespoons fresh thyme, chopped
2 garlic cloves, crushed
salt and freshly ground black pepper

Fennel & Feta with Pomegranate Seeds & Sumac

This is a lovely simple salad – goes with anything or just have a big bowl on its own. I think my friend, Fi Potter, gave me this among many other lovely recipes she has passed on to me. You can make it more substantial for a supper dish and add some slices of cooked chicken and some roasted pine nuts, should you wish.

Serves 4

1 tablespoon pomegranate seeds
2 medium fennel heads
1½ tablespoons extra-virgin olive oil
2 teaspoons sumac
juice of 1 lemon
2 tablespoons flat-leaf parsley, roughly chopped
100g feta, crumbled
salt and freshly ground black pepper

Remove the leaves of the fennel, keeping a few to garnish later, and trim the base, making sure you leave enough of it still attached to hold the slices together. Slice very thinly lengthwise.

In a bowl, mix the olive oil, sumac, lemon juice, parsley and some salt and freshly ground black pepper. Add the fennel and toss well. Taste for seasoning but remember the feta will add saltiness.

Layer the fennel, then the feta and then the pomegranate seeds. Garnish with fennel leaves, sprinkle over some sumac and serve immediately.

Greek Salad

A really lovely simple Greek salad recipe, which goes well with moussaka, grilled chicken or roast chicken with lemon and oregano – or just on its own with some good bread. You do not really need to be specific about the exact amount of the ingredients, but when in Corfu we obviously had a lot of Greek salads and so when we had the most perfect one up at Thomas' Restaurant Foros in Old Perithia, I actually asked his wife for an exact recipe and here it is. She did not use cherry tomatoes, but tasty tomatoes from her garden.

Chop and cut all the tomatoes.

Slice the onion very finely and add to the tomatoes.

Slice the deseeded cucumber and green pepper into thin slices and add to the tomatoes and onion.

Roughly chop the dill, mint, black olives and add them to the salad.

Mix the red wine vinegar with the salt, freshly ground black pepper and olive oil and toss it in the salad.

Sprinkle on the oregano and the feta cheese.

Serves 6

3 medium tomatoes
200g ripe cherry tomatoes
1 medium red onion
1 cucumber
1 green pepper
1 handful chopped fresh dill
1 handful fresh mint
1 handful black olives

Dressing
1 tablespoon red wine vinegar
3 tablespoons good quality Greek (if possible) olive oil
salt and freshly ground black pepper
200g feta cheese
1 teaspoon dried oregano

Sides & Salads

Dad Baker's Pickled Onions

My father's delicious pickled onions, which he made every year – although a pain in the neck peeling all those onions! It helps if you bring them to the boil in a pan of boiling water, then remove and peel once they have cooled down sufficiently to handle. This is one of the recipes I don't expect people other than my nephews, nieces and my son to be interested in, but I wanted to include it for the nostalgic record!

Makes enough for 4 medium-sized Kilner jars

2kg baby onions, peeled and sprinkled with salt
1 litre malt vinegar
250g demerara sugar
1 teaspoon mixed spice

Warm the vinegar with the sugar and spice – bring to scalding not boiling. Pour this over the onions whilst hot. Leave the onions to infuse for 24 hours – then drain off the spiced vinegar.

Bring the spiced vinegar to boiling point in a saucepan and then pour back over onions.

Keep in sterilised Kilner jars.

Quinoa, Camargue Red Rice, Pistachio & Dried Cherry Salad

This is an unusual salad – you can leave the dried cherries out if you like, or you could replace them with pomegranate seeds. If you don't like quinoa do use bulgur wheat instead.

Bring to the boil two saucepans filled with salted water and simmer the quinoa and rice separately. The first for 13 minutes and the second for 22 minutes. Drain both, refresh under cold water, and leave in fine sieves to drain.

While the grains are cooking, fry the onion in a little olive oil until golden brown. Allow to cool.

In a bowl, mix cooked grains with all the other ingredients and season with salt and pepper generously. Serve at room temperature.

Serves 2

100g quinoa or bulgur wheat
100g Camargue red rice
½ onion, peeled and sliced
3 tablespoons light olive oil, plus a little extra for frying
zest of 1 orange
juice ½ orange
1 teaspoon lemon juice
½ garlic clove, crushed
2 spring onions, thinly sliced
50g dried cherries, halved
30g pistachio nuts, lightly toasted and roughly chopped
20g rocket leaves
salt and freshly ground black pepper

Roasted Sweet Potato or Butternut Squash with Roasted Red Onion & Tahini

This is a simple salad recipe and is a good starter, light lunch or supper dish. We have served it at many a winter wedding and it is always popular and looks beautiful on the plate with the colour of the sweet potato or butternut squash and red onions.

Serves 4

3 large sweet potatoes, peeled and chopped into chunks
2 red onions, cut into quarters
50ml light olive oil
3½ tablespoons light tahini
1½ tablespoons lemon juice
2 tablespoons water
1 small garlic clove, crushed
30g pine nuts, roasted
1 teaspoon zatar
1 small bunch flat-leaf parsley, chopped
salt and freshly ground black pepper

Preheat the oven to 200°C.

Toss the sweet potato and red onions in 2 tablespoons of the light olive oil and salt and then bake in oven for about 40 minutes until soft and brown. Take out of the oven and leave to cool.

Make the tahini sauce by whisking the tahini with the garlic, lemon juice, water and a good sprinkling of salt until the sauce is the consistency of single cream.

Spread the cooled vegetables over a flat serving platter and then drizzle over the tahini sauce followed by the pine nuts.

Roasted Crispy Kale or Cavolo Nero

This is such a wonderful way of serving kale. You can buy a bag of ready chopped kale from any supermarket, but do be aware that you will need to go through the bag and take out any coarse stalks which have been left in. I find it easier to buy un-chopped kale or cavolo nero and just take each long stalk out. It is so wonderful with roast chicken or slow cooked lamb or any roast really. I gave this to my young niece, Lucie, recently who until then hated kale – she absolutely loved it this way.

Preheat the oven to 150°C.

Wash the kale well and then destalk it. Dry the kale well and then put it all in a big mixing bowl and massage the light olive oil into it and sprinkle it with salt.

Line a large baking tray or two small trays with Bakewell paper and spread the kale on to the tray.

Roast in the preheated oven for about 20 minutes or until crisp.

Serves 6

1kg kale
3 tablespoons light olive oil
1 teaspoon sea salt

Shona's Tabouli

I love this and used to eat it at the wonderful Lebanese restaurant in Brook Green – Chez Marcelle. Sadly, Marcelle retired a few years ago and I wish I had asked her for her recipes before she did! I have made this up and it is as close to her tabouli as I can work out. The more chopped parsley you put in the better, but don't overdo the mint as it can make it too sharp.

Serves 6

40g bulgur wheat
40g flat-leaf parsley, chopped
10g mint, finely chopped
8 on-the-vine cherry tomatoes
juice of 2 lemons
2 tablespoons extra-virgin olive oil
1 teaspoon sea salt

Cook the bulgur wheat in boiling water for 8 minutes and drain thoroughly and let it cool.

Chop the cherry tomatoes and put them in a bowl with the lemon juice and olive oil. Mix in the salt, parsley and mint and cooled bulgur and give it a good stir.

Simple Delicious Kale Salad

This is so surprisingly good that, even though it sounds odd, do try it as it is completely delicious and very healthy. It is very important to really massage in the dressing as this softens the kale nicely – you could add some chopped avocado and pomegranate seeds to make it more substantial if you like.

Take the kale out of the bag and take out all the hard bits of stem.

Wash kale and dry thoroughly in a salad spinner.

Mix the tahini, light olive oil, cider vinegar and lime juice together with a good pinch of salt.

Massage the dressing into the kale with your hands (you can do it with plastic gloves) for about 5 minutes until the kale wilts and is all well covered with the dressing.

Serves 4

250g chopped kale
1 tablespoon light olive oil
1 tablespoon tahini
1 teaspoon cider vinegar
juice of 1 lime
salt

Sweet Potato Mash

This is a wonderful alternative to normal potato mash – you could also make it with butternut squash or parsnips or celeriac. I have also made it with butter instead of olive oil and just added a spoonful of crème fraîche which is equally as good.

Serves 6

6 large sweet potatoes, cut into large chunks
4 tablespoons light olive oil or 25g butter
good pinch of freshly grated nutmeg
good pinch of cayenne pepper
a knob of butter

Boil the sweet potato until tender, about 15 minutes, then drain really well.

Mash with the rest of the ingredients.

Tomato Sauce with Baked Feta

I made this recipe up after having eaten it at a delicious little restaurant in Kassiopi, Corfu years ago. It is a lovely vegetarian option.

Serves 6

Preheat the oven to 200°C.

Bake the tomato halves in oven with olive oil, balsamic vinegar, honey, garlic, chilli and thyme for 30 minutes.

Blitz the whole lot in a food processor and add the tomato purée and salt and freshly ground black pepper.

Place the tomato sauce in an ovenproof baking dish or 6 individual ramekin type dishes, sprinkle the feta on top and bake for 10–15 minutes.

1kg ripe plum tomatoes, halved
4 tablespoons light olive oil
2 tablespoons balsamic vinegar
3 tablespoons runny honey
4 garlic cloves, finely chopped
2 teaspoons dried chilli flakes
5 sprigs thyme
3 tablespoons tomato purée
salt and freshly ground black pepper
250g feta

Uncle Jack's Dhal

I love recipes that remind me of special people. I spent most of my 20s hanging around with the Elias family – my favourite of whom was Uncle Jack, a really special person who died at a ripe old age last year. This is his simple recipe for dhal which his daughter, Fi Potter, gave me.

Serves 6

170g red split lentils
1 large onion
2 teaspoons garam masala
½ teaspoon turmeric
½ teaspoon crushed garlic
1 large garlic clove sliced
½ teaspoon ground black pepper
salt

Slice and fry onion till golden brown, for 10 minutes approx.

Add garam masala, turmeric, garlic and pepper and fry for 2–3 minutes.

Add split lentils, cover with water until it is 5cm above the lentils, add salt and freshly ground black pepper and boil with lid on pan, until soft.

Fry garlic slices briefly so they don't burn and put on top of the dhal and serve.

Wiz's Light Weekly Salad Supper

My friend, Wiz Deakin, makes this salad for supper most nights for her and her wonderful husband Tom, and it is truly delicious and so simple.

Just chop or tear the chicken breast into bits and add in a bowl with the salad, chopped avocado, goat's cheese, grapes cut in half, the basil and beetroot, then stir in the dressing – it makes a lovely messy and delicious salad.

Serves 2

1 cooked chicken breast (or buy one from Waitrose)
1 bag watercress, spinach and rocket
1 avocado
150g soft goat's cheese
1 large bunch red seedless grapes
a few fresh basil leaves
2 small beetroot, ready cooked and cubed
1 tablespoon homemade French dressing
granary toast to mop the whole lot up

Two Feta-Based Salads

These are both wonderful salads. Either have them on their own with some pitta bread or have them with griddled lamb cutlets or griddled chicken. Always buy the best feta you can get – I buy mine from the Iranian supermarkets in Shepherd's Bush or the one near the Robin Hood Roundabout on the way to Kingston.

First Recipe

Serves 6

½ cucumber
1 spring onion or small red onion, finely sliced
10 cherry tomatoes, cut into quarters
½ red chilli, deseeded and finely chopped
150g flat-leaf parsley, roughly chopped
60g feta
3 tablespoons light olive oil
salt

Cut the cucumber lengthways and then spoon out the seeds. Finely chop the flesh of the cucumber and put in the bowl you are going to serve it in.

Add the onion, cherry tomatoes, chilli and flat-leaf parsley.

Crumble the feta separately and add the olive oil – mix well together to make a thick feta dressing. Mix this all into the salad with your hands (with plastic gloves if you are worried). Taste for salt.

Second Recipe

Serves 6

1 x 400g tin chickpeas, drained and rinsed
1 large red onion, finely chopped
1 tablespoon light olive oil
2 tablespoons extra-virgin olive oil
3 garlic cloves, very finely chopped
1 red chilli, deseeded and finely chopped
4 spring onions, finely chopped
30g flat-leaf parsley, finely chopped
25g coriander, chopped
juice of 1 lemon
250g feta, crumbled

First of all, fry the red onion in the light olive oil for 10 minutes until it is soft and then add the chilli and garlic and continue to fry for a minute, being careful not to burn the garlic, as it tastes horrid burnt. Leave to cool totally.

Put the chickpeas, spring onions, flat-leaf parsley and coriander into the bowl you are going to serve the salad in and then add the cooled onion mixture.

Add the feta to the bowl together with olive oil and lemon juice and stir very well until you have the most wonderful rustic salad – taste for seasoning and add salt if necessary.

Asian Slaw

This is a lovely slaw and quite different from coleslaw – I like it with slow-roast pork or even citrus-baked salmon.

Serves 4–6

1 red onion, finely sliced
500g white cabbage, finely sliced
200g red cabbage, finely sliced
2 yellow peppers, deseeded and finely sliced
1 papaya or mango, peeled and sliced
1 tablespoon mint, chopped

Dressing
3 tablespoons white wine vinegar
2 tablespoons lemon juice
100ml rapeseed or sunflower oil
2 tablespoons sesame oil
4 tablespoons light soy sauce
3 tablespoons light soft brown sugar

Mix the dressing ingredients together and then mix with all the vegetables and papaya or mango, add the mint. All done now and yum! It is so good.

Chicken Stock

I always have homemade chicken stock in plastic takeaway containers in my freezer – I would be completely lost if we ever ran out! We roast so many whole chickens that I often have carcasses left. If I don't happen to have any, my butcher always has some going begging – so it is worth asking your butcher. I always say to people, just use water if you don't have any fresh stock.

Makes about 1 litre

2kg chicken bones/carcasses
2 large onions, peeled
3 large carrots, chopped
4 celery stalks
10 black peppercorns
2 bay leaves
10 parsley stems
4 litres water

Preheat the oven to 200°C.

Put the chicken bones/carcasses on a baking tray and roast for 20 minutes until well browned.

Put the bones, vegetables, peppercorns, bay leaves, parsley stems and water into a large pan and bring to the bubble on top of the stove – turn the heat down to low and bubble for 1½ hours to 2 hours. Do not let it boil too hard – just keep it at a simple bubble.

After the time has elapsed – sieve the stock through a fine sieve and let it cool before freezing in little containers until you need to use it.

Easy Savoury Pastry

I have put a sweet shortcrust pastry recipe in the puddings section but thought I should put this one in the savoury section as well. There is another easier recipe below, but they are both good.

Makes enough for 1 large tart tin – 32cm approximately

275g plain flour
150g butter, cubed
½ teaspoon sea salt
2 large egg yolks
1 pudding spoon iced water

Preheat the oven to 180°C.

Put the flour, butter and a pinch of salt into your food processor bowl. Pulse until it is all blended. Add the two egg yolks and the iced water. Keep pulsing until it binds and then take it out of the mixer and wrap it in cling film. Put it in the fridge for 20 minutes or so until the pastry has firmed up.

Take it out of the fridge and roll out so that it is big enough to fill a loose-bottomed 32cm tart tin.

Once in the tin, prick the base and cover with baking paper and baking beans. Put back in the fridge for 10 minutes and then put in the hot oven for 15 minutes until the pastry is golden brown.

Very Easy Pastry

I use this simple recipe for all my savoury tarts. Joan Fabian gave it to me years and years ago in Zermatt when she came to stay in the chalet I was working in.

Preheat the oven to 180°C.

Melt butter in pan over low heat and then stir in the flour and water.

Push the mixture into a loose-bottomed 32cm tart tin – pushing it down so it is quite thin and making sure it goes up the sides. Put into a fridge to set and then bake blind in oven for about 15 minutes.

Makes enough for 1 large tart tin – 32cm approximately

280g butter
450g plain flour
1 pudding spoon water

Aubergine, Feta & Broad Bean Salad

This is a great light lunchtime summer salad served with good pitta breads or any fresh bread. If you can't find the broad beans, frozen peas would work as well. This is also nice served alongside some griddled thin little lamb chops.

Serves 6

2 tablespoons light olive oil
3 large aubergines, cut lengthways and chopped
150g fresh or frozen broad beans
1 red onion, thinly sliced
juice of 1 lemon
2 tablespoons extra-virgin olive oil
250g on-the-vine cherry tomatoes
1 tablespoon fresh mint, chopped
2 tablespoons flat-leaf parsley, chopped
200g feta, crumbled

Preheat the oven to 180°C.

Toss the aubergines in the light olive oil and a sprinkling of salt and then put on a lined (with non-stick paper) baking tray and bake for about 35 minutes until nicely browned. Take out of oven and leave to cool.

Bring a pan of salted water up to the boil – add the broad beans and bring back to the boil and simmer for 1 minute. Drain well and cool and then pop the broad beans out of their skin.

Put the broad beans, the onion, the cherry tomatoes, the fresh herbs and the olive oil into a large bowl and add the lemon juice. Add the aubergines and feta and give a good old stir. Season to taste with salt and pepper – don't forget the feta is salty itself.

Kale Pesto

I love this as an alternative to the usual basil pesto – such a lovely supper dish and so easy to do. I am trying to put in as many vegetarian recipes as I feel fit, as so many people are now going vegetarian including my oldest friend, Peako, who I went to school with 50 years ago and has specifically asked me to put in extra vegetarian recipes.

Remove the stalks from the kale or cavolo nero and bring a large pan up to the boil. Add some salt, the kale and garlic cloves and blanch for 2 minutes. Drain well.

Cool a little. When cool put the leaves and garlic into a food processor and pulse to a purée – then add the olive oil to make a lovely dark green purée. Season very well with salt and pepper.

Cook the pasta in a large pan of boiling salted water as per packet instructions – usually about 10 minutes – drain well and then add the sauce until the pasta is well coated. Serve in individual bowls or plates and sprinkle with the grated Parmesan.

Serves 4

1kg kale or cavolo nero
4 garlic cloves, peeled
250ml extra-virgin olive oil
500g pasta of your choice
4 tablespoons finely grated Parmesan

Rocket & Pistachio Pesto

Another delicious pesto.

Serves 4

2 garlic cloves, crushed
½ teaspoon salt
60g shelled pistachios
60g rocket
40g Parmesan, grated
250ml light olive oil
500g pasta of your choice

Crush garlic cloves in a pestle and mortar if you have one with the salt until creamy.

Put the nuts into your food processor and pulse until coarsely chopped – then add the rocket and pulse until you have a paste.

Mix the paste with the garlic, grated Parmesan and oil.

Tip You could keep it covered in the fridge for several days if you like but bring up to room temperature before using with cooked pasta.

Chickpeas with Aubergines & Tomatoes

It is so useful to have tins of chickpeas in your cupboard or better still, dried ones, but you have to remember to soak them overnight before cooking them. This is a lovely recipe – comfort food and good to mop up with some really good flatbreads and maybe a dollop of Greek yoghurt. A great vegetarian supper or as a side dish to some lovely slow cooked lamb or lemony roast chicken.

Preheat the oven to 180°C.

Line 2 large baking trays with non-stick paper.

Cut the aubergine into chunks and toss in 2 tablespoons of the light olive oil and salt. Put on the baking trays and bake for 40 minutes in the oven until nice and brown.

Put the remainder of the olive oil into a heavy-based casserole dish and gently fry the onions for 10 minutes until nice and soft.

Add the spices, sugar and garlic and give a good stir.

Add the two tins of cherry tomatoes and the water and bubble for about 30 minutes until the sauce is nice and thick.

Add the chickpeas and cook for another 10 minutes before adding the aubergines and serve.

Serves 6

3 large aubergines
4 tablespoons light olive oil
salt and freshly ground black pepper
2 onions, peeled and finely sliced
2 garlic cloves, crushed
2 x 400g tins cherry tomatoes
1 x 400g tin chickpeas, drained
275ml water
1 teaspoon sugar
1 teaspoon cumin
¼ teaspoon ground cinnamon

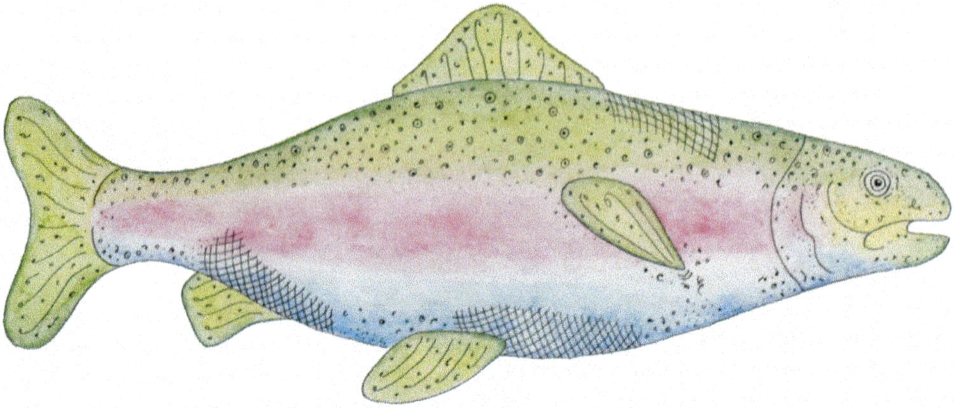

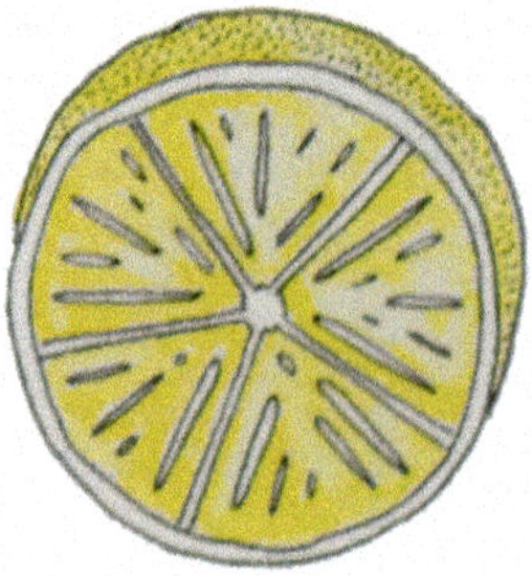

Fish

A Modern Take on Kedgeree

I was given this recipe by a client and asked to cook it for the fish eaters at her wedding. It always worries me when people give me a recipe I have not tried before but this one was a huge success, so I feel I must put it in my book as it is delicious. I am afraid that I don't know where Lily (the Bride) got it!

Serves 4–6

- 1 large onion, finely chopped
- 15g butter
- 1 tablespoon light olive oil
- 3 teaspoons good curry powder
- ½ teaspoon turmeric
- ½ teaspoon ground ginger
- pinch cayenne pepper
- ½ teaspoon ground cardamom
- 125g new potatoes, cut into chunks
- 100g bulgur wheat
- 1 litre homemade chicken stock
- salt and freshly ground black pepper
- 150g Puy lentils
- 1 bay leaf
- 50ml single cream
- 500g undyed smoked haddock fillets, skinned and cut into chunks
- 1 small bunch coriander, chopped

Warm the butter and olive oil in large heavy saucepan. Fry the onion gently until very soft – at least 10 minutes.

Add the curry powder and spices and cook for another couple of minutes.

Add the potatoes, bay leaf and stock and simmer for 10 minutes – then add the bulgur and simmer for another 10 minutes until the bulgur and the potatoes are cooked.

In another saucepan, cover the lentils with water but no salt (the salt would harden them in cooking) and cook for 25 minutes, testing to see if soft before draining. Then add to the potatoes, bulgur and stock.

Finally add the chunks of haddock to the mixture and bubble until the fish is cooked – only about 2 minutes – and then stir in the chopped coriander.

Baked Cod with Oregano & Lemon Potatoes

I love this dish; a great chef in Corfu served it to me once and I have cooked it several times since for friends when they come for dinner. You do need good thick fresh fillets.

Preheat the oven to 180°C.

Peel and slice the potatoes lengthwise into 4 and put them into a roasting dish in a single layer.

Put the onion and garlic in with the potatoes and oregano. Mix in the lemon juice and olive oils and bake the potatoes in the oven for 1 hour, giving them a good stir now and again.

Leaving the potatoes in the oven, turn up the temperature to 200°C.

Put the fish in a buttered oven dish – skin side down – shake over some olive oil (not too much) and bake for 15 minutes.

Serves 4

Potatoes
1kg waxy potatoes
225g onions, peeled and finely chopped
4 garlic cloves, peeled and chopped
1 bunch fresh oregano or 1 tablespoon dried oregano
100ml light olive oil
100ml extra-virgin olive oil
juice of 3 lemons
sea salt and freshly ground black pepper

Fish
1kg thick fillet of fresh cod, skin-on
light olive oil
salt and freshly ground black pepper

Baked Parcels of Salmon with Fresh Herbs

This is such an easy way to cook salmon – you can either wrap each piece individually as the recipe says, or you could lay the salmon pieces into an ovenproof dish and cover with Bakewell paper and cook that way. Delicious served with crushed new potatoes with some baby spinach stirred through. I used to serve this when I was doing Directors lunches in the City about 30 years ago – the days when most companies had cooks in to do their lunches. Now I think mostly it is all done by contract caterers.

Serves 6

6 salmon fillets
juice of 1 lemon
4 tablespoons light olive oil
4 tablespoons chives, chopped
salt and freshly ground black pepper
1 leek
2 small carrots
1 extra tablespoon lemon juice
125g butter, melted

Mix the lemon juice, oil, half of the chopped chives and a seasoning of salt and freshly ground black pepper.

Pour this mixture over the salmon in a large shallow dish and leave to marinate for 1 hour.

Trim the leek into matchsticks and do the same with the carrots. Place in pan of boiling water and blanch for 1 minute – drain well.

Put the melted butter in small saucepan and then put the leeks in and toss them around and soften them over a gentle heat.

Preheat the oven to 180°C.

Cut 6 squares of non-stick baking paper large enough to enclose each salmon fillet.

Brush each sheet with a little olive oil and place the salmon piece in the centre and top with a spoonful of the vegetable mixture. Draw opposite sides of the paper square over the fish and fold closed, then fold the ends underneath to make a neat parcel.

Arrange parcels in one layer in a baking dish or on a baking tray.

Put salmon in oven and bake for 15–20 minutes.

Warm the remaining butter with the tablespoon of lemon juice and add the rest of the chopped herbs.

Open up the parcels and transfer the salmon to hot serving plates.

Pour over the melted lemon butter.

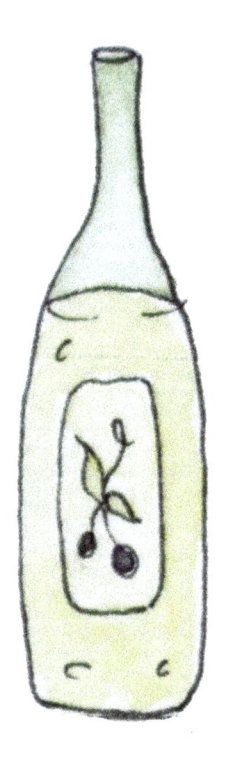

Braised Seafood Provençal with Fennel

A really simple fish dish for supper or lunch – you could use any firm filleted fish you like. I do buy my fish from an excellent fish shop; if you don't have a good local one, I would recommend the Waitrose fish counter.

Serves 6

- 4 tablespoons of light olive oil
- 1 onion, finely chopped
- 1 fennel, finely chopped
- 2 garlic cloves, crushed
- 2 sprigs thyme or ½ teaspoon dried thyme
- 60ml dry white wine
- 1 x 400g tin peeled plum tomatoes
- good pinch of dried chillies
- 300ml fish stock or water
- 225g monkfish fillet
- 150g cod or hake fillet
- 150g swordfish or tuna
- 2 tablespoons fresh parsley, chopped

Heat the oil in a frying pan and add the onion – fry gently for 10 minutes.

Add the fennel slices and cook for a few more minutes, then add the thyme and garlic.

Add the white wine and reduce by half.

Stir in the tomatoes and crush them with the back of a spoon – simmer for 30 minutes until you have a lovely rich tomato sauce.

Cut all the fish into smallish chunks and then add to the tomato sauce – simmer for 5 minutes and season with salt and pepper to taste.

Serve sprinkled with parsley.

Fish Soup / Stew

I have just made this today for a client and she is going to add the fish to the sauce later this evening and hopefully not overcook it! You can use any seafood – whatever is fresh and in abundance.

Serves 6–8

1 onion, finely chopped
2 carrots, finely chopped
2 celery sticks, finely chopped
1 leek (white only), finely chopped
2 garlic cloves, crushed
2 tablespoons light olive oil or rapeseed oil
400g cherry tomatoes, cut in half
1 x 400g tin peeled cherry tomatoes with their juice
600g new potatoes (preferably Cyprus or Cornish or Jersey), cleaned and chopped to the same size as the tomatoes
2 bay leaves
½ teaspoon allspice
1 litre fish stock or 500ml fish stock and 500ml water
1 teaspoon light soft brown sugar
salt and freshly ground black pepper
750g fresh cod, boned and skinned
750g scallops
750g large prawns, skinned
750g monkfish or sea bass
juice of 1 lemon
1 small bunch flat-leaf parsley, roughly chopped

Fry the onion very gently for about 10 minutes in the oil in a large pan and then add the carrots, celery and leek for another 5 minutes before adding the garlic.

Add the chopped tomatoes and the tin of tomatoes to the pan and give a good stir.

Add the stock/water and season well.

Bubble the sauce on the stove for 10 minutes before adding the bay leaves, light soft brown sugar and allspice. Put a lid on the pan and cook for another 20 minutes.

Cut the fish into even-sized pieces and add to the pan and then simmer for another 10 minutes until the fish is just cooked through.

Add the chopped parsley and the lemon juice.

Haddock with Herb & Walnut Crust

Such an easy and quick haddock dish – you could also do it with cod or any thick white fish. Lovely served with some new potatoes in season with lots of parsley, butter and some fine green beans.

Serves 6

6 fillets of haddock (about 200g each)
70g fresh white breadcrumbs
50g flat-leaf parsley
1 shallot, chopped
35g walnuts, toasted
60ml walnut oil

Preheat the oven to 180°C.

Put the breadcrumbs, parsley and shallot in a food processor, process to mix. Add toasted walnuts and pulse gently.

Add the walnut oil.

Place the fish fillets on a lined baking tray and spread the breadcrumb mixture on top of each piece and cook in the oven for 8 minutes.

Butter Roasted Cod with Spring Onion Mash

I always cook fish on non-stick baking paper, and then it's easy to move on to your plate once cooked without breaking it to pieces. Spring onion mash goes so well with fish.

Serves 6

Preheat the oven to 200°C.

Cook the potatoes in a large pan of salted boiling water – time them for 20 minutes and drain. Let them dry before mashing with olive oil and freshly ground black pepper. Add the spring onions.

Put the fish on a baking tray lined with baking paper, dot with the butter and sprinkle on lemon zest. Season and put in the very hot oven for exactly 10 minutes – if the cod is thin it could take only 8 minutes – so do check after 8 minutes.

2kg King Edward or Maris Piper potatoes
200g cod fillets
30g butter
zest of 1 lemon
2 bunches spring onions, trimmed and sliced thinly
3 tablespoons light olive oil
sea salt and freshly ground black pepper

Roasted Monkfish with New Potatoes & Wilted Spinach

This really is so easy and delicious – one of my very favourite and oldest friends, Peako, cooked it for us when we first visited them in their lovely new home in Scotland. She kindly sent me the recipe and I have done it several times since. Monkfish is expensive but worth it.

Serves 4

2 thick monkfish fillets (350g each)
750g new potatoes, scraped clean
300g baby leaf spinach
2 tablespoons olive oil
85ml extra-virgin olive oil, plus extra to serve
balsamic vinegar
salt and freshly ground black pepper to serve

Preheat the oven to 200°C.

Season the monkfish with some salt and set it aside for 15 minutes.

Cook the potatoes in well-salted boiling water until tender.

While the potatoes are cooking, heat the olive oil in a large ovenproof frying pan.

Pat the monkfish dry on kitchen paper, add to the pan and sear for 3–4 minutes. It is important not to move it when it is browning on each side.

Transfer the pan to the oven and roast for 10–12 minutes, until the fish is cooked through but still moist and juicy in the centre.

Remove from the oven, cover with foil and set aside for 5 minutes.

When the potatoes are done, drain them well and return them to the pan with the extra-virgin olive oil. Gently crush each potato against the side of the pan with the back of a fork until it just bursts open.

Season the potatoes and add any juices from the fish.

Add the spinach leaves and turn over gently until they are well mixed in.

To serve

Cut the monkfish across into thick slices. Spoon the crushed potatoes onto warm plates and put the monkfish on top. Put your thumb over the top of the bottle of extra-virgin olive oil and drizzle a little around the outside edge of each plate. Do the same with the balsamic vinegar and then sprinkle over a few flakes of sea salt and coarsely crushed black pepper.

Salmon with Spring Onion Noodles

I have had this recipe for years – given to me by my lovely friend who is an excellent cook, Issy Entwisle. It never fails to work and people always love it. It can be served cold as a part of a buffet or lunch, or good taken on a picnic. Basically it is a very versatile dish!

Serves 4

3 tablespoons dark soy sauce
4 tablespoons caster sugar
juice of 1 lime
5 tablespoons sunflower oil
150g thread egg noodles
4 x 125g skinless salmon fillets
salt and freshly ground black pepper
4 teaspoons Chinese five spice powder
125g spring onions, cut into thin strips
125g celery, cut into thin strips
125g cucumber, halved lengthways, deseeded and cut into strips
coriander sprigs to garnish

Place the soy sauce and sugar in a small saucepan, bring to the boil then remove from the heat. Stir in the lime juice and 4 tablespoons oil then set aside.

Roughly break the noodles and place in a bowl. Cover with boiling water, soak for 4 minutes and then rinse and drain.

Season each salmon fillet with salt and pepper and the five spice powder. Heat the remaining oil in a large non-stick frying pan, add salmon and cook for 3 minutes each side.

Toss the noodles in the soy dressing with spring onions, celery and cucumber.

Arrange on plates, top with a piece of fish and garnish with coriander.

Tamarind Fish Curry

I love recipes that remind me of special people – this one was given to me by Fi Potter who has exactly the same taste in food as I do and it is so simple and really delicious. You can find tamarind paste at any Asian shop near you if you live in a city. If not, you could order it online from Amazon.

Cut the salmon into chunks and set aside.

Slice the onion and fry gently in vegetable oil until soft for about 10 minutes.

Grate ginger on a large grater. Add to the pan with the chopped garlic and stir into the onion mixture.

Add ground coriander, cumin, turmeric and chillies.

Add tamarind, tomato purée, coconut milk, sugar and heat.

Simmer uncovered for 10 minutes.

Add fish chunks and cook for a few minutes.

Scatter with coriander. Serve with rice.

Serves 6

750g salmon fillets
1 teaspoon sea salt
1 red onion
1 tablespoon vegetable oil
2cm fresh ginger, peeled and grated
3 cloves garlic, peeled and finely chopped
1 teaspoon ground coriander
1 teaspoon ground turmeric
pinch of cumin
2 small chillies or 1 large, finely chopped
1 tablespoon tamarind paste
1 tablespoon tomato purée
1 x 400g tin of coconut milk
1 teaspoon sugar
10g fresh coriander leaves

Sumac & Citrus Baked Salmon

This dish is quick to prepare and nice with red or black rice with some walnuts and perhaps chopped coriander tossed through. You can have it hot or it is equally good served cold with some lovely salads.
Sumac is a Middle Eastern spice – I think originally from Iran, made from dried and ground sumac berries. You can get it from most supermarkets and if not, from an Iranian shop, if you have one near you.

Serves 6

6 salmon fillets
2 teaspoons sumac
½ teaspoon ground cumin
½ teaspoon ground cinnamon
grated zest and juice of 1 orange
grated zest and juice of 1 lime
3 tablespoons of light olive oil
salt and freshly ground black pepper

Preheat the oven to 180°C.

Mix the sumac, cumin, cinnamon, orange zest and juice and lime zest and juice with the olive oil. Pour over the salmon fillets.

Season with salt and pepper and bake for 12 minutes.

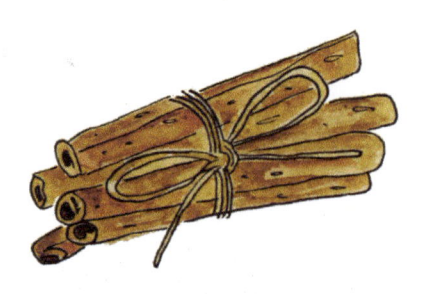

Simple Massaman Fish Curry

This is a simple curry which, as long as you buy a good curry paste, you can make easily and it cannot go wrong. The brand I buy from the local Thai shop in Hammersmith is Mae Ploy. You could easily serve this at a dinner party with some jasmine rice. Make it with any firm white fish – monkfish holds its shape the best, but it is expensive.

Heat the oil in a casserole dish with a heavy base and fry the onion gently for 10 minutes until very soft. Then add the ginger and garlic and fry gently for another few minutes.

Add the curry paste and cook for another couple of minutes, then add fish stock, water or chicken stock.

Add the coconut milk and bring to a gentle simmer – add the sugar and salt.

Once it is hot and simmering but not boiling too fast, add the fish and simmer for another few minutes until it is cooked.

Add lime zest and juice to taste.

Serves 6

1 tablespoon vegetable oil
1 onion, peeled and finely sliced
2 garlic cloves, crushed
4cm fresh ginger, peeled and finely chopped
2 tablespoons Massaman curry paste
300ml water or fish stock or even chicken stock
1 x 400ml tin of coconut milk
2 teaspoons light soft brown sugar
¼ teaspoon salt
750g cod, haddock or monkfish fillets
400g large raw prawns, peeled
zest of 1 lime
juice of 2 limes

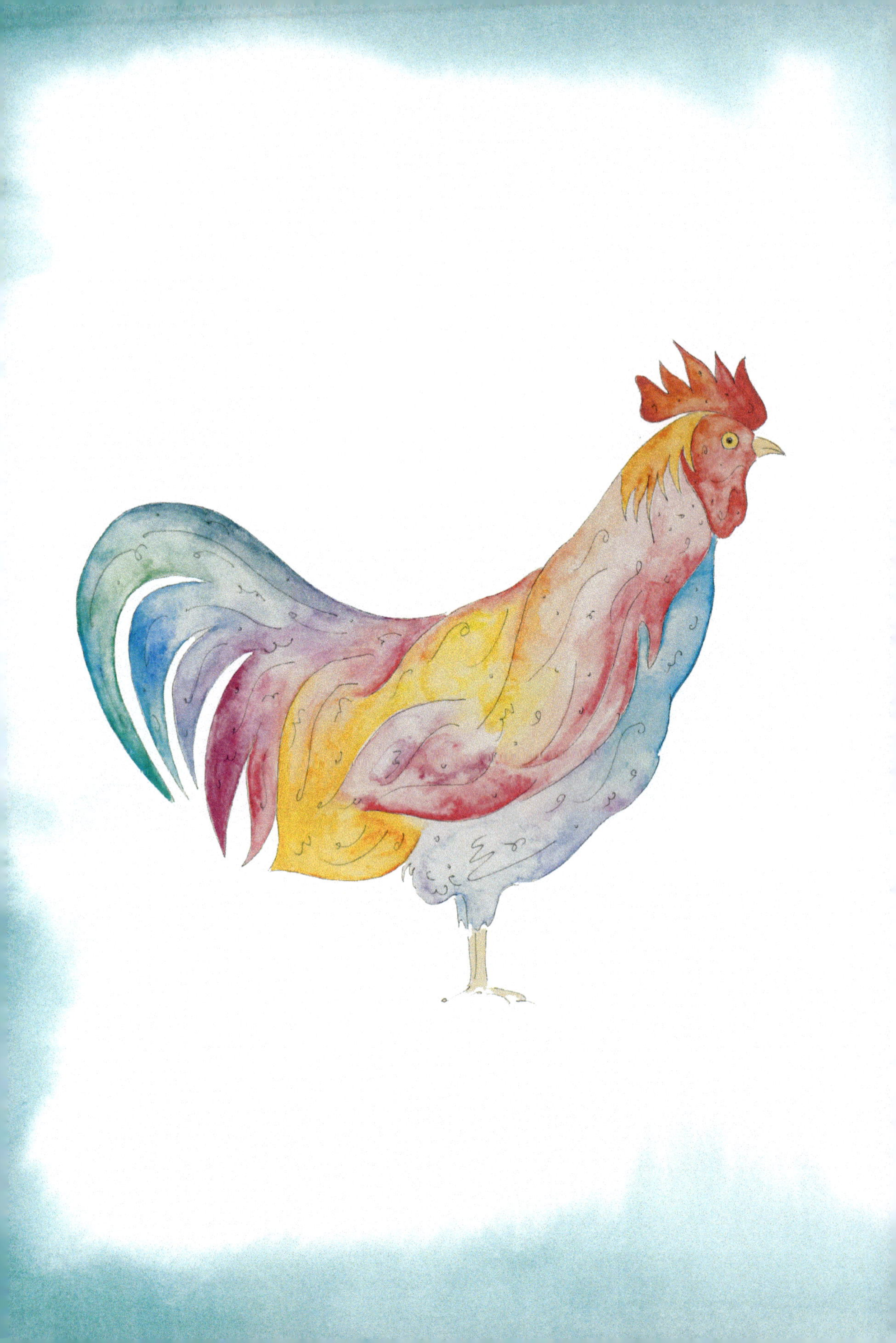

Chicken

Barbecued Chicken Thighs

This recipe is an adaptation from a barbecued pork recipe my old friend, Georgie Fry, served up to me many years ago when she first moved to the country. I think she got it from those old Cordon Bleu recipe magazines, but it is still really good and so simple. Probably not that healthy but worth it! I use the marinade when asked to do teenagers' parties – it makes for delicious chicken skewers. Cut the chicken thighs in chunks and just marinate them in the mixture and bake in the oven. You can also use pork fillet instead of the chicken thighs.

Serves 4

8 large chicken thighs
40g butter
2 tablespoons soy sauce
1 tablespoon Lea & Perrins Worcestershire sauce
4 tablespoons tomato ketchup
1 tablespoon HP Fruity Sauce
1 tablespoon runny honey
1 tablespoon Dijon mustard
salt and freshly ground black pepper

Preheat the oven to 180°C.

Brown the chicken thighs in the butter on top of the stove, or in the oven in a baking dish. Cook them slowly until they are a lovely crusty brown colour.

Mix marinade ingredients together and pour over chicken in baking dish. Bake in oven for 40 minutes until chicken is cooked.

Serve with plain boiled rice.

Chicken Baked with Parmesan & Herbs

This is one of my favourite chicken dishes – you can use trimmed chicken thighs on the bone with skin on, or a breast with skin and a bit of bone (known in the trade as Supremes). It is also nice cold and taken on a picnic – I keep mentioning picnics as I just love a picnic or an evening beach barbecue. I adore eating outside!

Serves 4

8 skin-on chicken thighs, or 4 skin-on breasts with a bit of bone
4 large garlic cloves, crushed
3 medium eggs
2 heaped tablespoons fresh parsley, finely chopped
2 heaped tablespoons chives, finely chopped
2 heaped tablespoons thyme, finely chopped
50g of fresh breadcrumbs
40g Parmesan, grated
50g butter
4 tablespoons light olive oil
salt and freshly ground black pepper

Marinate the chicken for 4 hours
First of all put the chicken bits in a dish large enough to hold them in one layer. Place the garlic cloves with 1 heaped teaspoon of salt in a pestle and mortar and crush to a purée. Add this to the beaten eggs and season with some salt and pepper. Whisk well with a fork before pouring the whole lot over the chicken and leaving to marinate for 4 hours – turning the chicken over halfway through.

Preheat the oven to 180°C.

After 4 hours combine the breadcrumbs, Parmesan, parsley and a little seasoning together on a plate. Spread some absorbent kitchen paper on a flat surface.

Remove chicken from fridge and take one piece at a time and carefully sit it in the crumb mixture – patting the mixture carefully over it.

Pop a shallow roasting tin with the butter and olive oil in the oven.

Once the fat is very hot, remove the tin from the oven and put the pieces of chicken in and baste them well and cook for 20 minutes.

Then turn over the chicken and cook for another 20 minutes before finally pouring off the excess fat from the tin and giving them another 5 minutes.

Chicken Chasseur

This is the first recipe I learnt at cookery school in 1976 – it is so delicious and people love it. You can use boned and skinned chicken thighs or boned and skinned chicken breasts but thighs are much nicer and never dry out like breasts can. If you don't mind dealing with chicken bones I find it even tastier using chicken thighs with their bones left in. It is still a very popular dish when people ask me to cook traditional food for their wedding. I like it served with a good mash or some lovely baby new potatoes scrubbed clean and sprinkled with chopped parsley and a good dollop of melting butter.

Melt the butter in a heavy-based pan, add the bacon and fry gently until crisp. Remove bacon from pan.

Dredge the chicken pieces in flour and fry until brown.

Add herbs, garlic and seasoning and put bacon back in pan.

Add wine and mushrooms.

When the wine starts to bubble add the tomato purée and simmer for 45 minutes.

Serves 4

8 chicken thighs, or 4 free-range chicken breasts
250g dark field mushrooms, sliced
4 slices streaky bacon, chopped
1½ pints white wine
1 tablespoon flour
60g butter
3 garlic cloves, crushed
fresh thyme
1 bay leaf
1 tablespoon tomato purée
salt and freshly ground black pepper

Chicken, Leek & Tarragon Pie

During Covid lockdown when all our weddings were cancelled, I started doing deliveries to all my clients and this was the most popular of all the dishes we delivered. Sometimes I poach the chicken but if you find that a fiddle, you can just roast it in an oven at about 170°C for 1.5 hours with a bit of water at the bottom of the pan and let it go cold as you do for the poached version.

Serves 6

1 medium chicken
6 leeks
1 bunch tarragon, chopped
1 bunch flat-leaf parsley, chopped
60g butter
60g plain flour
500ml chicken stock
salt and freshly ground black pepper
8 black peppercorns
220g shop-bought ready rolled puff pastry
1 large egg, beaten

Poach a whole chicken in water with the green parts of the leeks, peppercorns and salt. Once the pan has come up to the boil turn the heat down so the chicken gently simmers for an hour.

Drain the chicken, keeping the water/stock to make the sauce.

Take all the meat off the chicken and set aside. Boil up the stock to reduce it by a third.

Gently fry the finely sliced white parts of the leeks in the butter until soft.

Stir in the flour and then add about 500ml of the poaching liquid.

Stir in chopped tarragon and parsley and season with salt and pepper.

Preheat oven to 200°C. Cut the pastry to the size of your dish.

Place chicken mixture in pie dish and cover with ready rolled puff pastry. Prick the pastry and brush with beaten egg and then bake for about 30 minutes until golden brown.

Chicken Marinade

This is the marinade I made up for chicken and it is absolutely delicious. You can either marinate cubes or whole chicken thighs. Cubes are great for a canapé and the whole pieces make for an excellent supper. You could serve it with some boiled rice and maybe a peppery watercress salad. Liz Halls really urged me to put the recipe in.

To make the marinade – put all the above ingredients into the bowl of a food processor and pulse until you have a smooth mixture.

Marinate the chicken for a couple of hours.

Preheat the oven to 180°C and then spread the meat over a Bakewell paper-lined oven tray and cook in the oven for about 40 minutes until browned and cooked through. Delicious!

8 boned and skinned chicken thighs
100g bag fresh coriander
2cm fresh ginger, peeled and coarsely grated
1 green or red chilli
1 tablespoon runny honey
2 tablespoons vegetable oil
1 teaspoon sesame oil
1 tablespoon water

Chicken Thighs with Oregano & Pomegranate Molasses

This recipe was given to me by a client, Catharina Mannerfelt, for whom I cook regularly. You could serve it with a good Greek salad and some lovely new potatoes.

Serves 4

8 chicken thighs with skin on and bone in
2 tablespoons light olive oil
sea salt
500g red onions, finely sliced
4 garlic cloves, crushed
2 tablespoons pomegranate molasses
3 tablespoons light soy sauce
1 tablespoon runny honey
1 teaspoon freshly grated ginger
1 small bunch fresh oregano or 1 teaspoon dried oregano
50ml water

Preheat the oven to 180°C.

Heat oil in frying pan and brown chicken thighs – 4 at a time. Don't overcrowd pan so they brown nicely and don't stew. Once brown remove from pan and set aside.

Fry the onion until soft – about 10 minutes – add the garlic to the pan and fry for one minute.

Mix the garlic and onion with the chicken and then add the molasses, soy sauce, honey, ginger and oregano.

Add the water and then put the whole lot into a baking dish. Cover with foil, roast for 30 minutes and then remove the foil and bake for another 15 minutes.

Chicken with Yoghurt & Spices

This is a favourite chicken recipe. One of my clients gave it to me a few years ago and asked me to cook it for her daughter's 21st birthday party – we tried it and changed things a bit and since then have served it at many weddings. It is always so popular.

Serves 4

2 tablespoons light olive oil
8 chicken thighs, skinned and boned
2 onions, finely sliced
1 teaspoon ground cumin
½ teaspoon cayenne pepper
¼ teaspoon chilli flakes
4 garlic cloves, crushed
400ml chicken stock
250g full-fat Greek yoghurt
1 tablespoon cornflour
seeds from ½ pomegranate

Heat the olive oil in a broad, heavy-bottomed saucepan.

Season the chicken and brown on both sides until pale gold. Remove from the pan and set aside.

Add the onion to the pan and cook until soft and a very pale gold. Sprinkle on the cumin, cayenne pepper, chilli and garlic and cook for a couple more minutes.

Put the chicken pieces back in the pan, together with any juices and add the stock. Bring to the boil then immediately turn down the heat very low. Cover and cook for 20 minutes, then take off the lid and leave to cook for a further 15 minutes.

Mix the yoghurt with the flour. Add a small ladleful of the cooking liquor to the yoghurt and mix well. Now add the yoghurt to the pan and mix carefully. Gently heat through.

Scatter with the pomegranate seeds.

Chicken, Wild Rice & Red Grape Salad

This is good if you have leftover chicken from a roast. We often have it watching television on a Sunday night.

Serves 6–8

- 300g wild, red and basmati rice mix
- 600ml chicken stock
- salt and freshly ground black pepper
- 750g leftover cooked chicken, cut into broad strips
- 60g unsalted pistachios
- 4 tablespoons flat-leaf parsley, chopped
- 200g rocket, watercress or baby spinach
- 4 handfuls of red grapes

Put the rice into a saucepan and cover with the stock. Bring to the boil, season, then reduce the heat to a simmer. Cook until all the stock has been absorbed and the rice is tender. If it gets too dry, add a little water. It will take 25–30 minutes. Remember, wild rice never goes soft, it remains firm and nutty.

Meanwhile, make the dressing by simply whisking everything together. Taste for seasoning.

As soon as the rice is ready, pour on half the dressing and mix well so it absorbs the dressing while still warm. Leave to come to room temperature.

Toss in everything else, together with the rice and the remaining dressing. Taste for seasoning: rice dishes need a lot.

Coq au Vin Best Recipe

We have tried so many different Coq au Vin recipes and put several together to get the best result, so here goes. The most important factor I believe is to reduce the wine before using it – so many recipes omit to tell you that, which results in the finished dish having a bitter taste. Best cooked the day before and left in fridge overnight and then reheated.

To prepare the wine put the wine ingredients into a pan and bring to the boil – reduce the wine by half its volume over a medium heat and then strain through a sieve and reserve for cooking the Coq au Vin later.

Chicken

Season the thighs with salt and freshly ground black pepper and roll them in the flour.

Heat oil and butter in a heavy pan and sauté the chicken until golden. Remove chicken to a plate.

Fry the pancetta in the same fat until it is crisp. Remove and put with chicken.

Serves 4

Wine for cooking
1 bottle of decent red wine
4 sprigs thyme
2 bay leaves
1 tablespoon redcurrant jelly
1 small onion, peeled and stuck with 2 cloves
2 celery sticks
1 carrot, chopped
4 garlic cloves, peeled and bruised

Chicken
8 chicken thighs, on the bone but skinned
salt and freshly ground black pepper
1 tablespoon plain flour
20g butter
1 tablespoon light olive oil or sunflower oil
75g of pancetta, cut into thick cubes
20 small shallots
20 button mushrooms or 10 field mushrooms

Fry the shallots in the same pot until brown and remove.

Fry mushrooms until soft and then put all the chicken, pancetta, mushrooms and shallots together in the pot.

Pour over the wine and cook for an hour in 160°C oven, or if you prefer, on a low heat on top.

Coronation Chicken

There are so many mucked-up Coronation Chicken recipes but here below is the original one I learnt 45 years ago. It is delicious. Please don't be tempted to add anything like raisins to it – it completely spoils it.

Serves 4–6

1 medium chicken
300ml mayonnaise
150ml whipped cream or crème fraîche

Wine sauce/base
a dollop of light olive oil
2 shallots or 1 small onion, finely chopped
1 pudding spoon medium curry powder
1 teaspoon tomato purée
150ml red wine
1 bay leaf
salt and freshly ground black pepper
2 tablespoons apricot jam or mango chutney

Poach or roast the chicken. To poach the chicken, put it in a saucepan with water to cover, a bay leaf, half an onion, a chopped carrot, some whole peppercorns and bubble for an hour. Leave the chicken in the poaching liquid to cool. To roast the chicken, preheat the oven to 180°C, put the chicken in a roasting pan with a little water at the bottom and roast in oven for 1 hr 15 minutes or until cooked.

Make the wine sauce – fry the chopped onion in the olive oil until soft for about 10 minutes – do not let it burn – add the curry powder and fry gently for a few more minutes. Then add the tomato purée, red wine, bay leaf, apricot jam, salt and freshly ground black pepper. Simmer this for 20 minutes and then strain through a fine sieve and leave to cool.

Once the base is cool, mix in the mayonnaise and whipped cream or crème fraîche.

Tear the cooked chicken and stir it into the mayonnaise, cream and red wine curry mixture. Season to taste.

Roast Chicken with Paprika, Cayenne Pepper & Thyme

There are so many things you can add to a chicken when you are roasting it – this is the nicest one I have done so far and I served it with roasted cauliflower and butternut squash.

Serves 4

1 medium chicken
40g softened butter
1 teaspoon mild paprika
¼ teaspoon cayenne pepper
salt and freshly ground black pepper
4 sprigs thyme, leaves taken off, or ½ teaspoon dried thyme

Preheat the oven to 180°C.

Mix together the butter, paprika, cayenne pepper and thyme.

Rub the butter mixture all over the chicken.

Season with salt and pepper.

Cook in oven for 1.5 hours.

Simple Chicken Curry

This is the first chicken curry I ever cooked and I still do it very often. All you need to do is serve it with basmati rice and maybe some finely chopped tomato, red onion and cumin with a squeeze of lemon. There are many chicken curry recipes out there but whenever I do this for clients they are very complimentary about this particular recipe.

Serves 4

Preheat the oven to 180°C.

Dip the chicken pieces in the well-seasoned flour.

Heat the oil in a pan and brown the chicken all over and remove to a casserole dish.

Fry the onions until they are light brown (about 10 minutes), then add the garlic, cumin, turmeric and cook for 2 minutes.

Add the stock, bay leaf, tomato purée, lemon juice and mint.

Add salt and freshly ground black pepper.

Bring slowly to the boil, stirring continuously and then pour over the joints in the casserole dish and cook in oven for 50 minutes.

- 8 chicken thighs with bone and skin on or 4 large chicken pieces
- flour for coating, seasoned with a pinch of turmeric, cayenne pepper, dried English mustard powder and crushed coriander
- 30ml vegetable oil
- 2 medium onions, chopped
- 1 garlic clove, crushed
- 5ml cumin powder
- 10ml turmeric
- 290ml stock or water
- 1 bay leaf
- 10ml tomato purée
- juice of 1 lemon
- 30ml fresh mint, chopped
- 30ml fresh coriander, chopped
- 15ml cream
- 10ml plain yoghurt

Take out of the oven and immediately add the yoghurt and cream and stir in well.

Add the chopped fresh mint and coriander.

Golden Jubilee Chicken

Another cold chicken salad type recipe – good for picnics and summer lunches or suppers. This one someone served at a Golden Jubilee party, so I have called it that.

Serves 4

500g chicken thighs, boned and skinned
salt and freshly ground black pepper
½ teaspoon freshly grated nutmeg
2 tablespoons light olive oil
1 bunch flat-leaf parsley, roughly chopped

Marinade
zest and juice of 1 lime
3cm fresh ginger, grated
1 garlic clove, crushed or finely chopped
2 tablespoons light olive oil

Dressing
100ml crème fraîche
6 tablespoons mayonnaise
zest and juice of 1 lime
5cm fresh ginger, grated

Mix all the marinade ingredients together and add the chicken – cover and refrigerate for a couple of hours.

Preheat the oven to 170°C.

Make the dressing by mixing all the ingredients together in a bowl.

Scrape the marinade from the chicken and pat dry with kitchen paper. Season the chicken with salt, pepper and nutmeg and place in roasting tin. Drizzle the olive oil over the chicken. Roast in the oven for 25 minutes until the meat is cooked through.

Leave the chicken to cool and cut it into bite-sized pieces.

Combine the chicken and dressing and refrigerate until needed.

Indonesian Marinated Chicken with Roast Sweet Potatoes & Peppers

I always love this dish and serve it simply with basmati rice. You can buy the Sambal Oelek online at Amazon or at your local Asian supermarket if you are lucky enough to have one near you – it's not easy to find in the regular supermarkets.

Serves 4

8 chicken thighs, boned and skinned

For the marinade
1 onion, quartered
2½cm fresh ginger
2 tablespoons runny honey
6 tablespoons light soy sauce
2 tablespoons Sambal Oelek (Indonesian hot chilli paste)
juice of 2 limes

For the potatoes
3 sweet potatoes, peeled
1 red onion
2 red peppers
2 garlic cloves, crushed
1 tablespoon olive oil
1 tablespoon balsamic vinegar
salt and freshly ground black pepper

To serve
125ml creamy Greek yoghurt
fresh coriander sprigs to garnish

Preheat the oven to 190°C.

For the marinade, put the onion, ginger, honey, soy sauce, Sambal Oelek and lime into a food processor and pulse to a coarse paste.

Pour this sticky marinade over the chicken, turning to coat each piece well. Cover and set aside while you prepare the vegetables.

Cut the potatoes, onion and peppers into similar sized chunks.

Place in a baking dish with the garlic, oil and vinegar. Sprinkle with salt and pepper and toss well so that every vegetable surface is well coated.

Roast in a baking dish until tender and slightly caramelised for about 40 minutes.

Meanwhile, put the chicken on a baking dish and roast in the oven for 40 minutes.

When the chicken and vegetables are ready put them on a large platter and sprinkle with the fresh coriander and yoghurt to serve.

Malaysian Chicken

This is one of the nicest Thai/Malay chicken curry recipes I have found – it looks complicated but it is not – you just need to get all the ingredients out first to make the paste and then you are halfway there. Nat Haywood gave me this recipe and it is really good.

Serves 6

Curry paste
5 garlic cloves, peeled and roughly chopped
4 red chillies, trimmed, deseeded and roughly chopped
5cm fresh ginger, peeled and chopped
4 large shallots, peeled and chopped
1 tablespoon finely chopped lemongrass
1 teaspoon ground turmeric
2–3 tablespoons groundnut oil

Curry
1kg skinless and boneless chicken thighs
2 tablespoons groundnut oil
2 onions, peeled and thinly sliced
salt and freshly ground black pepper
4 kaffir lime leaves (can leave these out if you can't find them)
1 cinnamon stick
3 star anise
1 x 400ml tin of coconut milk
100ml chicken stock or water
1 teaspoon light soft brown sugar
2 tablespoons light soy sauce
400g green beans, trimmed and cut into 5cm lengths
handful of coriander leaves, roughly torn

Make the curry paste first: put the garlic, chillies, ginger, shallots, lemongrass and turmeric in a food processor and whiz to a paste.

With the motor running, trickle in the groundnut oil and blend well, scraping the sides of the processor several times.

Cut the chicken into bite-sized pieces.

Heat the groundnut oil in a large cast-iron casserole or heavy-based pan.

Tip in the curry paste and stir over a medium heat for a few minutes until fragrant.

Add the onions and cook, stirring frequently, for 5 minutes until they begin to soften.

Season the chicken pieces with salt and pepper. Add to the pan and stir to coat them in the spice mixture.

Add the lime leaves, cinnamon stick, star anise, coconut milk, stock or water and soy sauce and bring to the boil.

Reduce to a simmer and cook gently for 30–40 minutes until the chicken is tender.

Skim any fat off the curry and add the green beans and cook for a few minutes.

Sprinkle with the coriander leaves and serve with basmati rice.

Mediterranean Chicken

I know how annoying I am about food and recipes – I can feel myself being so bossy and opinionated sometimes, especially as I am always asking people for recipes to keep! This recipe was served about 20 years ago at my friend, Margaret Andrew's, 50th birthday party in Richmond. I managed to get the recipe from her friend who cooked it for her and have done it several times since. It is brilliant for a summer picnic or summer lunch party – I served it at Ascot a few years ago for some very discerning, but lovely, clients of mine and they loved it!

Serves 10–12

Meat of 3 large cooked chickens
250ml extra-virgin olive oil
2 tablespoons fresh oregano, chopped (definitely not dried)
8 tablespoons fresh basil, chopped
juice of 2 lemons
1.5kg tomatoes
2 red peppers
2 red onions
2 yellow peppers
4 courgettes, sliced and roasted
salt and freshly ground black pepper

Preheat the oven to 180°C.

Firstly, prepare all the vegetables. Skin the tomatoes by putting them in a bowl of boiling water for a minute or two until you see the tomato skins bursting slightly – then take off the skins and remove the seeds and chop roughly.

Cut up the red and yellow peppers and deseed them.

Skin and cut the red onions into quarters.

Cut the courgettes into chunks.

Toss all the vegetables in 2 tablespoons of the olive oil and salt and pepper, and then spread out on two oven trays lined with non-stick baking paper.

Put in oven for about 30 minutes until well browned.

Let the vegetables cool and then mix in a large bowl with the chicken, the remaining olive oil, the lemon juice and chopped fresh herbs.

Moroccan Chicken

This is such an easy dish to prepare and nice and light. You could use chicken breasts if you prefer white meat, but thighs are more tender. It is lovely served with simple boiled rice.

Serves 4

500g chicken thighs, boned, skinned and cut into 2cm chunks
4 tablespoons flour, seasoned with salt and freshly ground black pepper
60ml sunflower oil
2 medium onions, sliced
2 teaspoons ground cinnamon
¼ teaspoon ground cloves
2 teaspoons sumac
4 tablespoons sultanas
250ml chicken stock
50g pine nuts, toasted
4 tablespoons coriander, chopped
juice of 1 lemon

Mix the chicken with the seasoned flour. Heat half the oil in a frying pan and cook until golden and set aside.

Heat the rest of the oil in the pan and fry the onions at a low heat for ten minutes.

Return the chicken to the pan, add the spices, sultanas and stock. Reduce the heat and cook slowly for about 25 minutes or until the chicken is cooked through.

Stir in the pine nuts, coriander and lemon. Serve with Greek yoghurt.

Bridget's Oven Chicken Bits with Thyme & Lemon

This is another excellent, simple recipe which Bridget Jackson gave me years and years ago. Just like me, she loves simple food. It is particularly good as you can leave it in the oven for a long time and have it for supper with a simple salad and a baked potato or some scrubbed new potatoes.

Serves 4

4 free-range chicken pieces on the bone (I like thighs)
3 tablespoons olive oil
4 garlic cloves
juice of 4 lemons
1 bunch thyme
2 sprigs rosemary
4 red onions
sprinkle of caster sugar
salt and freshly ground black pepper

Preheat the oven to 180°C.

Season the chicken pieces and put in a roasting tin.

Pour over enough olive oil to moisten them (about one tablespoon).

Squeeze the lemon over the chicken and drop the empty lemon skins in too.

Sprinkle over fresh thyme and rosemary.

Sprinkle over sugar.

Skin and cut the onions into quarters and put in the roasting tin.

Pour over the remaining olive oil.

Roast for 45 minutes.

Serve with plain boiled new potatoes and a green salad – delicious.

Really Easy Quick Sticky Thai Chicken

This is so simple and as long as you have the ingredients around it could not be an easier supper to throw together. Serve with boiled rice and maybe some pak choi if you have it.

Serves 4

8 chicken thighs on the bone with skin on
2 tablespoons lemongrass finely chopped (or 'easy' lemongrass in tube!)
1 teaspoon dried red chilli flakes
20g light soft brown sugar
20ml fish sauce
20ml light soy sauce
1 tablespoon grated ginger

Preheat the oven to 180°C.

Place chicken, lemongrass, chilli flakes, sugar, fish sauce, soy sauce and ginger in a bowl and toss well.

Place the chicken in roasting tin lined with non-stick baking paper and put in the oven and bake for 40 minutes or until golden brown and well cooked through.

Rocket, Chicken & Pistachio (or Pine Nut) Tabouli

This is a lovely fresh salad – especially good for a light summer lunch. Another one Georgie Fry gave me at a ladies' lunch years ago. Any food Georgie cooks is always delicious and beautifully presented. She had a company selling tableware, and the dishes I bought from her have travelled around the country with me as lovely platters from which to serve my canapés.

Boil the bulgur wheat in a pan of boiling water for 10 minutes and then drain. Cool completely and make sure it is very dry.

Place the wheat, rocket, parsley, mint, tomatoes and pistachios in a bowl.

Add the chicken to the salad with the lemon juice, olive oil, pepper and salt and toss to combine.

Serves 4

20g bulgur wheat
250g cooked chicken
250g rocket leaves
40g flat-leaf parsley, chopped
20g chopped fresh mint
200g cherry tomatoes, quartered
60g shelled pistachios
3 tablespoons lemon juice
3 tablespoons olive oil
salt and freshly ground black pepper

Zanzibar Chicken

This recipe is from Liz Halls who has worked for me now for many years and is an invaluable member of the team. It is a great rustic dish to prepare in advance and serve for a lunch or supper party. It freezes and reheats beautifully. Delicious with lovely plain basmati rice.

Serves 4–6

2 tablespoons oil
a knob of butter
8–12 chicken thighs or breasts, skinned, or a whole chicken skinned
1 onion, finely chopped
1–2 garlic cloves, crushed
1 tablespoon finely grated ginger
½–2 red or green chillies, deseeded and chopped (reserve a teaspoon)
Seeds from 5 cardamom pods – put them into a pestle and mortar and crush well to a powder
2 teaspoons ground coriander
2 teaspoons ground cumin
1 teaspoon garam masala
4–5 tomatoes, skinned and chopped or 1 x 400g tin chopped tomatoes
1 x 400ml tin of coconut milk
10g chopped coriander to decorate
juice of 2 limes

Warm the oil and butter in a large frying pan and fry the chicken in batches until browned all over. Transfer to a plate. Do not overcrowd the pan or the chicken will poach rather than brown.

Add the onion to the pan, lower the heat, cover and cook until softened for about 10 minutes.

Add the crushed garlic, ginger and chilli, cook for 1 minute, then stir in the spices and cook for a further minute or two.

Add the tomatoes and cook until softening, then pour in the coconut milk and return the chicken to the pan. Season well, and simmer gently for 35–40 minutes or until the chicken is cooked through.

To finish, add the coriander, reserved teaspoon of chilli and a little lime juice. Serve.

Fatuma's Marinated & Fried or Oven-Baked Chicken

This is another simple recipe – one of the nicest chicken marinades I have tasted for a long time. I would use boned and skinned chicken thighs but if you don't like dark meat you could use chopped breasts. Fatuma's Tower is the most lovely place we stay in regularly in Shela, Lamu, Kenya. The food there is so fresh and simple.

Mix all the above ingredients (apart from the chicken) together well in a jam jar with a screw top and give a really good shake.

Pour the marinade over the chicken and leave in fridge for 30 minutes. Then you can either fry gently in a pan with some oil or bake in preheated oven at 180°C for 25 minutes for breast and 40 minutes for thighs.

Serves 4

- 2 garlic cloves, peeled and finely chopped
- 2 tablespoons light soy sauce
- 2cm ginger, peeled and grated
- 2 sprigs of fresh rosemary
- 1 teaspoon garam masala
- juice of 2 limes
- 4 tablespoons light olive oil or vegetable oil
- 8 chicken thighs, boned, skinned and chopped, or 4 chicken breasts

Really Good Chicken & Lime Noodle Salad

This is easy to make and a lovely light lunch or even supper dish. You can quite get easily rice vinegar, fish sauce and thin noodles from any supermarket.

Serves 6

200g thin thread noodles
1 medium carrot, sliced very thinly
1 red pepper, deseeded and sliced thinly
1 large cooked chicken
20g fresh mint leaves, torn
20g coriander, chopped
2 garlic cloves, finely chopped
1 large red chilli, deseeded and finely chopped
2 tablespoons rice vinegar
125ml fresh lime juice
80ml peanut oil
2 tablespoons light soy sauce or fish sauce

Soak the noodles in boiling water. When tender, drain well.

Take the chicken meat off the bone and shred well.

Mix the noodles in a large bowl with all the ingredients above and toss gently.

Easy Chicken Bake

I found this recipe the other day in an old magazine. We used to do this for supper parties in the early 1970s when we were all sharing flats around South Kensington and Gloucester Road – before people living in Central London even thought of living in Fulham or Battersea, let alone even further out!

Serves 6

1 medium chicken, roasted and cooled
500g broccoli
1 x 295g tin condensed cream of chicken soup
1 x 200ml crème fraîche (must have been cream or sour cream in the old days)
3 large tablespoons Hellmann's mayonnaise or similar
2 teaspoons lemon juice
1 heaped teaspoon medium curry powder
freshly ground black pepper
110g fresh breadcrumbs
50g butter
50g cheddar, grated

Preheat the oven to 170°C.

First of all, bring a pan of water up to the boil and blanch the broccoli stems quickly in the boiling water – 1 minute will do – then drain quickly in a colander.

Take all the meat off the chicken.

Mix the condensed chicken soup with the mayonnaise, crème fraîche, lemon juice, curry powder and black pepper.

Fry the breadcrumbs in the butter until golden brown.

Put the drained broccoli on the bottom of a baking dish or ovenproof dish – put the chicken on top of the broccoli then pour the sauce over the top. Add the fried breadcrumbs and cook in the preheated oven for 45 minutes. Serve with a simple salad.

Spiced Chicken with Feta & Herb Bulgur Wheat

This is another lovely chicken salad lunch or supper type dish. Easy to make and very simple and fresh. When I use chicken breasts I always buy the ones with a little bit of bone and skin on – the fillets from a supermarket are not really good for something like this dish.

Serves 4

4 chicken supremes (about 125g each)
2 teaspoons harissa paste
300g bulgur wheat
½ red onion, peeled and finely chopped
zest of 1 lemon
6 cherry tomatoes, quartered
200g feta cheese, crumbled
20g flat-leaf parsley, roughly chopped
10g fresh mint, roughly chopped
3 tablespoons olive oil
salt and freshly ground black pepper

Preheat the oven to 180°C.

Rub the harissa all over the chicken. Put the chicken in a baking dish in the hot oven and roast for about 25 minutes until cooked through.

Bring a pan of water to the boil and boil the bulgur for 10 minutes; drain and cool. Once cool, put the bulgur in a large bowl with the cherry tomatoes, red onion, lemon zest, parsley, mint, olive oil and salt and freshly ground black pepper. Give it a thorough stir and add the feta.

Place the bulgur salad on individual plates and top with the chicken.

Poussins with Parsley, Chive & Thyme Sauce

This is so simple and is an impressive dinner party dish. You could serve it with a creamy mash or, in the spring/summer, with lovely English new potatoes with even more herbs and some fine green beans.

Serves 4

2 tablespoons light olive oil
4 poussins (about 400g each)
grated zest and juice of 1 lemon
4 tablespoons good chicken stock
salt and freshly ground black pepper
2 tablespoons chives, chopped
2 tablespoons thyme, chopped
2 tablespoons flat-leaf parsley, chopped
150ml double cream

Heat the oil in a large pan and add the poussins and brown slowly on all sides. When well browned add the stock, lemon zest and juice and salt and freshly ground black pepper.

Cover the pan and simmer for 30 minutes until tender. Remove birds and put on a warmed serving dish and keep hot.

Add the herbs and cream to the pan and heat gently – check the seasoning and pour over the poussins. Serve.

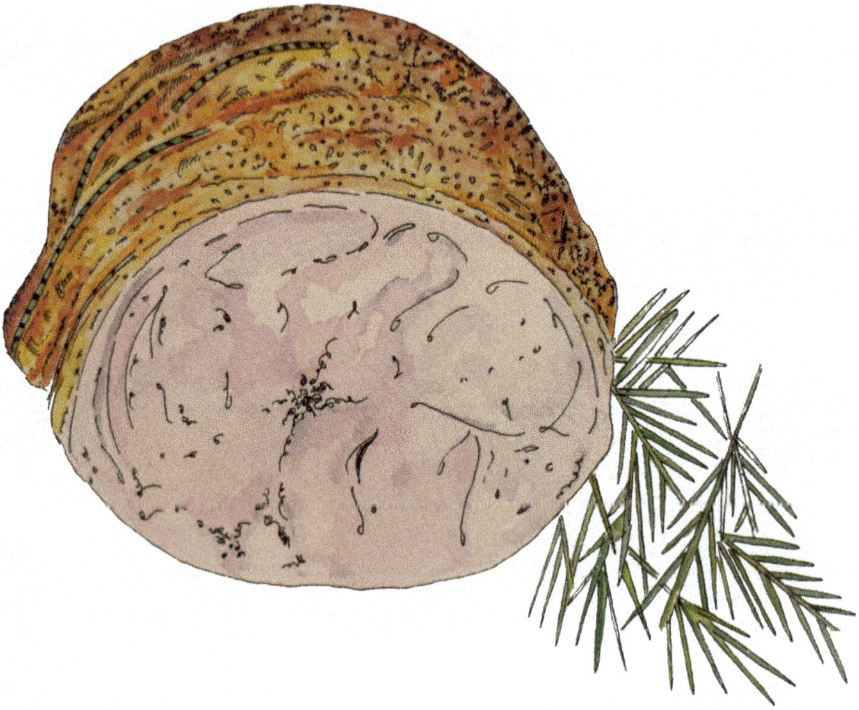

Pork

Auntie Kay's Baked Canadian Bacon

I have to put in this recipe in honour of my wonderful 'Auntie Kay', who all my friends knew and found amusing and lovely. Why it is called 'Baked Canadian Bacon' I don't know, but she always called it that. Gosh it is good though, albeit old-fashioned. Lovely served with mashed potato and cabbage with butter and black pepper. This is another recipe which is probably only in for my family!

Serves 6

1kg smoked gammon
50g soft light brown sugar
2 tablespoons Dijon mustard
500ml pineapple juice
300ml dry sherry
2 cloves
Le Creuset oven dish or similar heavy dish with lid to hold the gammon

Preheat the oven to 170°C.

Remove the skin from the gammon.

Score the fat side.

Combine sugar and mustard. Spread on gammon and stud with cloves.

Place in a Le Creuset oven dish or similar heavy dish with a lid. Pour juice and sherry round it.

Bake it for about 1.5 hours, basting occasionally.

Roast Pork Belly

I have tried so many different ways of doing belly of pork but this one definitely works the best – I like to serve it with mash and a green veg. Ask your butcher to score the skin of the belly or do it yourself with a Stanley knife. It is so important to get the pork from a really good butcher – do buy the best. Of all roasts, I think pork makes the best gravy. I always cook roast pork for my brother, Jono, who absolutely loves it!

Serves 4–6

1.5kg pork belly in one piece, skin on and scored
1 tablespoon light olive oil
150ml white wine
a splash of water (optional)
salt and freshly ground black pepper

Place the pork belly on a large board, skin-side up, and dry the skin thoroughly. Generously sprinkle with fine sea salt (about 1 tablespoon) all over the scored skin. Leave for half an hour, then dust off excess salt.

Preheat the oven to 220°C.

Transfer the pork to a large roasting tin greased with the olive oil and place in the hot oven on the top shelf. It is important that the oven is really hot to start with, as this intense heat is required to blister the skin and turn it into crackling. Roast at this high heat for a good 30 minutes until hard crackling has formed, then turn the heat down to 150°C and continue cooking for another 2–2.5/3 hours, until the meat is soft and tender.

Remove from the oven, transfer to a chopping board and leave to rest, loosely covered with foil to keep warm, for 15 minutes.

Meanwhile, make the gravy. Pour off any excess oil and place the roasting tray on the hob on a low to medium heat. Deglaze with the white wine, scraping the juices off the bottom of the pan as you go.

Simmer for a couple of minutes to reduce the alcohol, then taste for seasoning. If it tastes too strong, add a splash of water. Keep hot.

To serve the pork you can remove the ribs beforehand, as it is easier to slice.

Shoulder of Pork with Prunes & Cider

This is a delicious rustic dish – it really is good and simple, making a cosy supper when served with mashed potato and a green veg. The smell of it cooking is wonderful and warming – particularly on a dark winter's evening. I love the smell of the cider, prunes and balsamic vinegar bubbling away.

Serves 6

1kg shoulder of pork, cubed
450g shallot onions, peeled
2 tablespoons vegetable oil
40g butter
2 tablespoons flour
575ml dry cider
575ml chicken stock or water
1 tablespoon balsamic vinegar
250g pitted prunes
1 bay leaf
chopped parsley to decorate

Preheat oven to 150°C.

Put the onions into boiling water for a minute or so, then take them out and peel – leave them whole.

Warm the oil in a large casserole, add the butter and fry the pork pieces until well browned – a few pieces at a time. Remove the meat to a dish.

Add the onions to the pan and brown and then stir in the flour.

Add the cider and stock or water and bring to the boil.

Return the meat to the pan and add the prunes, salt, freshly ground black pepper and the bay leaf.

Cover and cook in oven for 2 hours until the meat is very tender.

Slow-Cooked Overnight Shoulder of Pork with Lemon & Chillies

As you will see from my recipes, I just love slow-cooked pork and I have chosen the best recipes for this book. Nicky Huntingford I have to thank for introducing me to this overnight method of cooking pork.

Serves 10

Preheat the oven to 220°C.

Put the garlic, salt, freshly ground black pepper and chilli flakes in a food processor with 1 tablespoon of the olive oil. Rub this mixture over the cut sides of the pork.

Put the pork in a low-sided baking tray in the very hot oven for 30 minutes until the skin begins to blister and brown.

3kg shoulder of pork; ask your butcher to score the skin really well
8 garlic cloves, peeled
salt and freshly ground black pepper
2 teaspoons red chillies, crushed
juice of 4 lemons
3 tablespoons light olive oil

Take out of the oven and pour over the lemon juice – turn oven down to 120°C and leave the meat to roast in the oven overnight, for a minimum of 8 hours and maximum of 16 hours.

When cooked, take the meat out of the oven and out of the pan. Leave to rest on a board and deglaze the pan with a bit of water to make a nice thin gravy.

Slow-Cooked Pig's Cheeks

This recipe is wonderfully easy to prepare and very economical – people are also very impressed with it as they have often not tried pig's cheeks. Thank you to Nat Haywood for this lovely recipe. Please don't be put off by pig's cheeks, they are delicious and soft to eat. I often recommend this recipe when people ask me to make them a casserole and they always say no, as I suppose pig's cheeks don't sound that appetising, but don't be put off!

Serves 4

8 pig's cheeks
50g butter
1 tablespoon light olive oil
1 carrot, finely chopped
1 medium onion, finely sliced
2 leeks, finely sliced
2 celery sticks, finely chopped
4 garlic cloves, finely chopped
1 bay leaf
250ml dry cider or apple juice
1 litre chicken stock
120g pancetta
1 Braeburn or Cox apple
400g peas

Preheat the oven to 140°C.

Brown the cheeks in butter – do 2 at a time so they don't steam but rather brown nicely.

Remove from the pan and then fry the onion and leeks gently for about 10 minutes until soft.

Add the carrot and celery and fry for another 5 minutes very gently.

Add the garlic, bay leaf, cider or apple juice and chicken stock.

Replace the pig's cheeks in the pan and place in oven for 4 hours.

Meanwhile fry the pancetta in a dry pan until golden – slice the apple and add to the pan. Add peas and 2 tablespoons of water and cook through until the peas are done.

Pork Chops with Dijon Mustard & Cream

I encourage my Brides to have pork as a main course as it is often overlooked and underrated. When I was a chalet girl in Zermatt in 1976, I was offered a lift back to London at the end of the season with a friend, Jilly Buckingham, and we drove all the way back in her Renault 4. I can't imagine how long it took! On the way we stopped at a wonderful little French hotel and had pork chops with mustard and cream and I can still see it now – so I have tried to do the recipe for you and here it is.

Serves 4

4 pork chops from a good butcher, about 2cm thick
salt and freshly ground black pepper
40g butter
1 tablespoon light olive oil
2 glasses of white wine, whatever's open
300ml double cream or crème fraîche
2 tablespoons Dijon mustard (Maille preferably)

Season the chops with salt and freshly ground black pepper – you will probably need two good frying pans on at the same time. Put the pans over a medium heat and divide the butter and light olive oil between them.

When the butter and oil are hot, add the chops – 2 in each pan – and brown each side. Then lower the heat and cook until the chops are cooked through – you could check with a sharp knife.

Remove the chops to a warmed serving dish and keep warm.

Pour off most of the fat from the pans – make sure you leave the delicious goo behind. Add a glass of white wine to each pan and bubble it up for a minute. Add the cream to each pan with the mustard and taste for salt and freshly ground black pepper.

Pour the sauce over the chops and serve with lovely mash and maybe some tenderstem broccoli.

Pork Loin with Chicory & Cider

Another lovely pork dish – not expensive and pork goes very well with chicory or endives, whichever you would like to call them. We used to cook this for guests in Meribel in 1975 when there were 9 chalet girls in total in the whole of Meribel. We made it up as pork loin was cheap at the local butcher and there was always chicory available in the little supermarket. I have cooked it ever since and it is very good and unusual.

Serves 4

750g rindless pork loin
a drizzle light olive oil
30g butter
6 chicory, remove the core at the bottom
4 shallots, finely chopped
400ml cider
2 sprigs sage if you have it
3 garlic cloves, peeled

Preheat the oven to 170°C.

Brown the pork loin in the oil in a heavy-based casserole dish until brown all over. Remove to one side.

Add the butter to the casserole and gently fry the chicory until they are browned – add the chopped shallots and mix everything together gently.

Put the pork back in and add the cider, garlic cloves and sage.

Cook for 30 minutes and then turn the pork over and cook for another 30 minutes.

Remove the pork, carve into thick slices and put on a serving dish with the sauce and chicory alongside.

Roast Shoulder of Pork with Star Anise, Soy & Cinnamon

Whenever I make this recipe, I think of a group of friends who all used to live in Singapore: Nicky Huntingford (my brother's first wife but always a sister-in-law to me), my sister, Sarina Graham and Fi Potter. When you buy the pork make sure you get it from a good butcher and ask them to score the skin really well. Included in the salads section is a recipe for Asian slaw which goes so well with this dish.

Serves 6

Preheat the oven to 220°C.

Put the star anise, cinnamon, whole garlic and ginger slices over the base of a good solid roasting tin.

Place the pork skin side up on top. Dry the skin really well with kitchen paper and rub the salt evenly all over the skin – immediately put the tray in the hot oven and cook for 30 minutes. This is to crisp the crackling.

Whilst this is going on, mix the sesame oil, light soy sauce, oyster sauce and brown sugar well together.

2kg boned shoulder of pork with skin on
4 star anise
3 cinnamon sticks
5cm fresh ginger, peeled and thinly sliced
5 garlic cloves, peeled
2 tablespoons sesame oil
200ml light soy sauce
100ml oyster sauce
4 tablespoons light soft brown sugar

Take the pork out of the oven and pour over the sesame mixture – turn the oven down to 150°C and cook the pork for 2½ hours.

Remove from the oven and let it stand for 15 minutes.

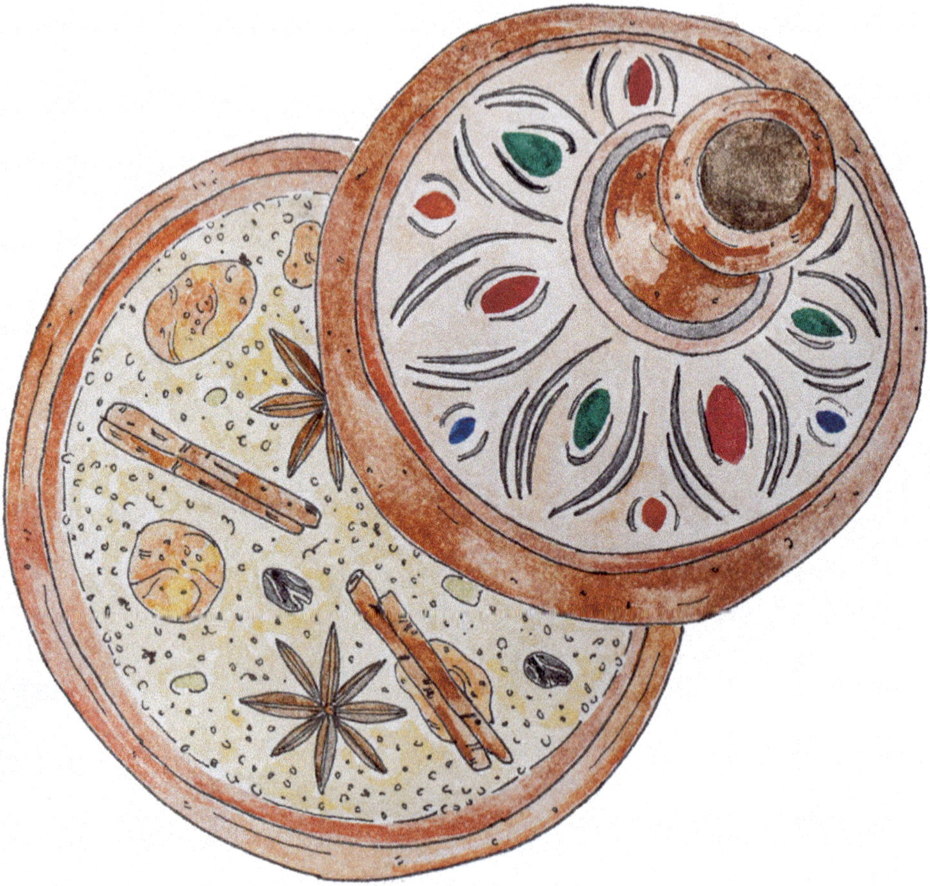

Beef & Lamb

Beef Stroganoff

This very simple stroganoff was the first meat dish we learned (meant to be very sophisticated) at my cookery school in London in the 1970s. Delicious and really worth doing. I know it sounds old-fashioned but this recipe has stood the test of time.

Serves 4

500g trimmed fillet of beef
1 medium onion, finely chopped
300ml white wine
150ml sour cream/crème fraîche
60g butter
1 tablespoon mild paprika
salt and freshly ground black pepper
250g chestnut mushrooms, sliced

Put the white wine in a small pan and boil for about 5 minutes until the liquid is reduced to about half the volume. Set aside.

Slice meat into strips and season with paprika.

Melt half the butter in pan, add onion and fry for about 10 minutes until softened. Remove from pan.

Add sliced mushrooms to the pan and fry for a few minutes until soft. Remove from pan.

Add remaining butter and when very hot, fry the meat quickly on high for 1–2 minutes.

Return the onion and mushrooms to the pan and add the reduced white wine and sour cream.

Carbonnade of Beef

Another old faithful – excellent with mashed potatoes and lovely crisp winter greens. Do buy good quality chuck beef from a butcher – this would be awful with over-trimmed stewing steak. Meat needs fat to make a good old stew.

Serves 4–6

Preheat the oven to 140°C.

Melt the dripping in a heavy pan and brown the meat in small batches – remove meat from the pan.

Fry the onions gently in the same fat – remove and drain the excess fat to a bowl.

Line a casserole dish with half the softened onion, half the meat, the studded onion then add the rest of the onions and meat, finishing with a layer of onions.

1kg chuck of good beef, cubed
5 onions, stud 1 with cloves, chop the rest
125g lard or dripping
2 teaspoons salt
½ teaspoon pepper
½ teaspoon freshly grated nutmeg
1 pudding spoon light soft brown sugar
1 pudding spoon flour
brown ale to cover (about 750ml)
1 tablespoon white wine vinegar

Sprinkle with the sugar, nutmeg and the vinegar. Season well.

Pour the fat back into the heavy pan and add the flour all at once – let the flour fry until light brown and add the ale (about 750ml). Stir well until it is a sauce consistency, then pour over the meat in the casserole to cover.

Cover the casserole with greaseproof paper and a lid and cook for 3 hours.

Goulash

Yet another delicious ancient recipe from cookery school. You can use beef, pork or lamb.

Serves 4

1 large onion, chopped
25g dripping or lard or butter
500g meat (as above), chopped
1 tablespoon paprika
2 teaspoons salt
freshly ground pepper
150g tomato purée
450ml fresh stock or water
2 tablespoons crème fraîche or sour cream
a few sprigs of thyme

Preheat the oven to 140°C.

Toss the chopped meat in the paprika.

Melt the fat in a heavy pan and brown all the meat in small batches – remove from pan.

Gently fry the onion for 10 minutes until soft and then put the meat back in pan.

Add the thyme and salt and pepper.

Dilute the purée with the stock or water and pour it over the meat.

Bring it to the boil, then lower the temperature and simmer for a minimum of 3 hours or in the oven for 3 hours.

Stir in the sour cream or crème fraîche just before serving.

Helen's Shoulder of Lamb

This is a brilliant and easy way of cooking a shoulder of lamb. I owe this recipe to my sister-in-law, Hels Baker, who has cooked it several times for me and I love it. Supper at her house is always delicious. One whole shoulder should do 6 people, depending on how big it is.

Serves 6

Preheat the oven to 150°C.

Put the lamb in an ovenproof dish with a lid, together with the lemons, oregano, rosemary and garlic.

Cover with greaseproof paper dampened and then the lid and cook for 4 hours.

1 shoulder of lamb with bone in
3 lemons, cut in half
1 bunch fresh oregano
2 sprigs fresh rosemary or thyme
4 garlic cloves

Lamb in Coriander

I have been doing this recipe for years and it never fails to please me. I found it in a magazine years and years ago.

Serves 6

- 1.5kg neck of lamb fillets, cut into 2cm slices
- 1 large bunch coriander or 5 x 15g packs
- 3 tablespoons sunflower oil
- 1 large onion, peeled and finely chopped
- 3 garlic cloves, crushed
- ½ teaspoon turmeric
- 1 level teaspoon ground cumin
- 500ml fresh chicken stock or water
- 200g frozen peas
- 1 large red or yellow pepper, thinly sliced
- salt and freshly ground black pepper

Put the coriander and stalks into a food processor with about 5 tablespoons water and whiz it up until you have a purée.

Heat 1 tablespoon oil in a casserole and fry the lamb until it is browned all over – add more oil if necessary.

Remove the meat from the pan and fry the onion and garlic for about 5 minutes in the remaining oil until they are soft.

Add the spices and the coriander purée and let the whole lot cook for about 5 minutes, stirring it so that it does not stick and burn.

Add the stock or water and meat, season and bring to the boil. Simmer uncovered for about 1 hour.

Once the lamb is cooked, add the frozen peas, red/yellow pepper and seasoning and cook everything for a further 10 minutes.

Lamb Meatballs with Tahini

I love this sort of food and have tried several different meatball/kofta recipes with my team as we sometimes do them for canapés. Paul Boarder (my main chef) has told me this one is his favourite. It is a mixture of many we have done! When having them for a supper or lunch I would serve them with some bulgur wheat or toasted flatbreads.

Serves 6

Preheat oven to 180°C.

Place everything other than the olive oil in a blender and blitz for a few minutes.

Make the mixture into oval shapes – about 4cm – and then lightly coat each ball with the olive oil – you can do this and leave them in the fridge to settle.

Place the meatballs on a lined ovenproof tray and bake for 15 minutes until just cooked through.

Tahini sauce Whisk all the ingredients together, adding water to achieve the consistency of single cream. Serve the sauce with the meatballs and sprinkle with toasted pine nuts.

800g lamb mince
1 onion, finely chopped
25g flat-leaf parsley, finely chopped
2 large garlic cloves, crushed
pinch dried red chilli flakes
1 teaspoon ground cinnamon
1 teaspoon ground allspice
freshly ground black pepper
1 teaspoon salt
2 tablespoons light olive oil

Tahini sauce

75ml tahini
2 tablespoons lemon juice
1 garlic clove, crushed
10g flat-leaf parsley, chopped
½ teaspoon salt
80ml water
30g pine nuts, toasted

Max's Fillet of Beef with Chilli & Coriander Dressing

This is my son, Max's, recipe which his friends always love and talk about.

Serves 6

20ml light soy sauce
black pepper
2½cm fresh ginger, grated
1 garlic clove, crushed
125ml vegetable oil
6 x 200g fillet steak
250ml rice vinegar
175g caster sugar
1 teaspoon salt
1 long red chilli, deseeded and chopped
4 tablespoons coriander, finely chopped

Mix the soy, black pepper, ginger, garlic and oil in a bowl.

Add the steaks and marinate for up to 2 hours in the fridge.

Put the vinegar and sugar in a saucepan and simmer for a couple of minutes over a low heat and then stir in the salt.

Cool the liquid.

Add the chilli and chopped coriander.

Take the steak out of the marinade and cook in a hot frying pan for one to two minutes each side.

Rest the steaks for a couple of minutes and then cut into cubes.

Drizzle the soy, pepper and ginger mixture over the steak and serve.

Moussaka

I had always made moussaka with lamb mince until I started going to Corfu every year, many years ago. I discovered there that they make it with either pork mince or a mixture of pork and beef mince. This really is a delicious recipe and I have included it for my sister, Nicky, as I suggested the other day, she use pork mice. She sounded sceptical but later called to say how delicious it was!

Serves 6

Preheat the oven to 170°C.

Slice the aubergine into 5mm slices. Sprinkle with salt and toss in a bowl with about 2 tablespoons of light olive oil.

Line a large baking tray with baking paper and put the aubergines in the oven until brown and crispy – about 40 minutes. Remove from the oven and leave to cool.

Heat 1 tablespoon of the oil in a wide non-stick saucepan. Gently fry the onion for about 10 minutes – be careful not to let it burn.

Add the parsley and garlic and cook for another minute until you can smell the garlic. Then add the mince.

Cook over medium heat until the meat loses its water and begins to brown.

2 large aubergines
about 3 tablespoons light olive oil
1 x 400g tin of tomatoes
125ml white wine
1 bay leaf
2 garlic cloves, crushed
1 teaspoon ground cinnamon
1 onion
3 tablespoons flat-leaf parsley, roughly chopped
850g minced pork and beef
½ teaspoon dried oregano

Sauce for topping
120g butter
120g plain flour
1 litre full-fat milk, warmed
a little freshly grated nutmeg
1 tablespoon freshly grated Parmesan

Add the cinnamon, oregano and bay leaf and season with salt and pepper.

When the mince is brown add the wine and scrape the bottom of the pan with your spoon to make sure no mince is stuck. Let most of the wine evaporate, then add the tinned tomatoes and leave it to simmer very, very slowly for about 1 hour or more.

Arrange half the aubergine over the base of your dish, slightly overlapping and half the mince. Add the rest of the aubergine, and then mince in layers.

Melt the butter in a saucepan. Whisk in the flour and cook for a few minutes, stirring constantly and then begin adding the warm milk.

When the sauce seems to be smooth and not too thick, add salt and pepper and a grating of nutmeg. Taste for seasoning.

Spoon over the mince.

Grate Parmesan over the top and bake for 45 minutes until bubbling and golden.

Rack of Lamb with Orange, Honey & Soy

I am pretty sure Vicky Hodgkinson gave me this recipe – any recipes she has are always wonderful and well thought through. She is a fabulous cook. There are many ways of doing rack of lamb and this is one of my favourites.

Make the marinade the day before and put the lamb with the marinade into two freezer bags – doubled up and leave in the fridge overnight.

Preheat the oven to 200°C.

Remove the lamb from the marinade and put in oven for 20 minutes.

Remove from the oven, pour over the marinade and roast for another 5 minutes.

Serves 4

2 French trimmed racks of lamb
220ml orange juice
2 tablespoons runny honey
2 tablespoons light soy sauce
2 tablespoons wine vinegar
2 garlic cloves, crushed
2 teaspoons dried rosemary
1 teaspoon ground ginger

General Meat Cooking Times

I thought it might be helpful to have the timings below – simple roasting times for you to look up when doing a roast.

Roast Beef

I use sirloin or rib of beef or even topside.

Always start it off in the oven with 'the hot sizzle', i.e. you put the joint into a very hot oven to sear the outside and then turn it down for the rest of the cooking.

Dust the outside of the joint with a mixture of flour and dry mustard and sprinkle with freshly ground black pepper (no salt as this encourages the juices to escape). Add a spoonful of beef dripping or ordinary olive oil to the tin and follow these timings:

For a joint up to 2kg – give it 20 minutes at 220°C. Then turn the oven down to 160°C and cook for another 10 minutes per 500g for rare, 15 minutes per 500g for medium and 20 minutes per 500g for well done.

Always take the meat out of the oven 15 minutes before carving and let it rest in a warm place. This is very important – it balances the temperature of the meat.

For a fillet, I always do the same thing: I buy a 2.5lb (1.10kg) fillet of beef (centre cut) and put it in a very hot oven at 200°C for 25 minutes. Before I put it in the oven I usually put a dollop of softened butter and some freshly ground black pepper on. Always take it out and sit it for 10 minutes. This gives really good, perfectly cooked rare beef.

Roast Pork

I always prefer roasting pork on the bone – leg, loin, belly or shoulder. Always go for larger joints – smaller ones can dry up.

2½kg joint would comfortably serve 6 people.

Always ask your butcher to score the skin well. Then leave the pork out at room temperature. Dry the skin with kitchen paper, cover with sea salt for half an hour – then wipe the skin again with kitchen paper to dry off the excess salt and any moisture it has drawn out of the pork.

Place in a heavy roasting tin and put in the oven for the 'hot sizzle': 220°C for 20 minutes; then turn the oven down to 160°C for 35 minutes per 500g. Don't forget to let it rest.

Roast Lamb

I use legs and shoulders – always with bone. My favourite way is again, to put the joint in the oven for 20 minutes 'hot sizzle' at 220°C and then turn the oven down to 160°C for 30 minutes per 500g.

The other way I love cooking lamb is just to put it in the oven for the 'hot sizzle' at 220°C and then turn the oven down to 110°C and cook the lamb for about 4 or 5 hours.

Tagine of Lamb with Mint, Apricots & Pine Nuts

This is such an old favourite of mine and I have been doing it for years; it is good served with either wild rice, bulgur, plain basmati rice or couscous, as set out below in the recipe. I always use neck fillet of lamb for braises or stews or tagines – it is lovely and sweet and easy to cook.

Serves 4

2 tablespoons light olive oil
1 large onion
1kg boneless lamb, cubed
450ml light meat stock
1 tablespoon wine vinegar
1 tablespoon runny honey
75g dried apricots, chopped
3 tablespoons fresh mint, chopped
50g pine nuts
salt and freshly ground black pepper to taste

Heat oil in large heavy-based pan and fry the onion gently for 10 minutes until lightly browned.

Add the lamb and stir well.

Add stock, vinegar, honey and apricots.

Bring to the boil, turn down the flame and cover and simmer for 1 hour.

Add the mint, pine nuts, salt and pepper and simmer for another 15 minutes.

Serve with hot buttered bulgur or rice with some pistachios and mint stirred through.

Griddled Lamb Cutlets with Sauce Paloise (Mint Hollandaise!)

I love lamb cutlets but they have to be very lean for me – fatty lamb is great for a slow-cooked recipe but when it comes to lamb cutlets, no fat please. I have learnt that the term for well-trimmed racks of lamb is 'Belgian trimmed', after having many a disaster ordering 100 or so racks of lamb for a wedding and being delivered racks with all the fat still on, which takes my chefs ages to trim.

I always laugh at 'Sauce Paloise' as so few people use the term these days. I was taught how to make it at my cookery school all those years ago. This would be delicious served in the spring with baby Jersey Royals with lots of butter and parsley and some fine green beans.

Serves 2

1 Belgian-trimmed rack of lamb
a drizzle light olive oil
pinch of salt

Mint hollandaise
5 egg yolks
3 tablespoons white wine vinegar
12 fresh mint leaves
250g butter, melted

I would make the sauce first and then tackle the lamb. Make sure the eggs are at room temperature and then put the egg yolks into the bowl of a food processor (keep the whites for making meringues – you can always freeze them).

Reduce the wine vinegar to 1 tablespoon in a small heavy pan over a medium heat – watch it so it doesn't evaporate completely.

Melt the butter and when still hot, turn on the food processor and whizz the egg yolks around. Very gently pour on the hot melted butter, with the motor still going – it should emulsify easily.

Then add the reduced vinegar.

Take the hollandaise out of the liquidiser and add the roughly chopped mint leaves.

Keep it warm/room temperature whilst you cook the lamb.

Chop the racks into chops: there should be 6 or 7 of them. Heat a griddle pan so it is very very hot – drizzle a bit of light olive oil over the lamb and griddle each side for 2–3 minutes, which will give you a delicious medium rare cutlet/chop.

Our Wedding Lamb

So many Brides and Grooms ask for lamb at their wedding and years ago we always served it pink – either a rack or a leg. But nowadays slow-cooked pulled lamb has become very popular. We sometimes put a shoulder of lamb on each table with a bowl of lovely Jersey Royals alongside, or we do it more Middle Eastern style with a tabouli to accompany it and some yoghurt with mint and garlic and a delicious Greek salad. Whichever way you serve it, it is always going to be very popular! I did this for my friend, John Clarfelt's, daughter Vicki's wedding, as it is his favourite dish and everyone seemed to love it.

Preheat the oven to 130°C.

Put the lamb in the oven all on its own with just a sprinkling of salt and pepper for 6 to 7 hours – the result is scrumptious.

You can take the lamb out and just bubble up the fatty sticky bits at the bottom of the pan with some white wine or stock and even a bit of flour, if you would like the sauce thickened.

Serves 8

1 large shoulder of lamb (about 3–3.5kg)
salt and freshly ground black pepper

Osso Buco Gremolata

During Covid lockdown, all weddings I cater for were postponed, so I decided to deliver to my local clients; it has proved a great success. This is one of the most popular dishes – some like it with lovely mash or a good Parmesan risotto. It is important you have a wide enough casserole dish so the veal pieces fit flat in the pan and not sit on top of each other.

Serves 6

1.2kg osso buco, 6 large pieces of veal shin
60g butter
2 tablespoons flour
1 onion, finely chopped
2 carrots, finely chopped
2 celery sticks, finely chopped
3 garlic cloves, finely chopped
200ml dry cider
200ml good chicken stock
1 x 400g tin plum tomatoes or passata
salt and black pepper
1 teaspoon sugar
2 sprigs thyme
light olive oil

Gremolata
4 tablespoons flat-leaf parsley, chopped
zest of 1 lemon
1 garlic clove, finely chopped

Preheat the oven to 150°C.

The first thing to do is coat the osso buco in seasoned flour – then melt the butter in a heavy frying pan and brown each bit on both sides until well browned. Remove from the frying pan and put in the casserole dish.

Once all the pieces are browned you may need to add a bit of light olive oil and then gently fry the chopped onion for about 10 minutes until lovely and soft.

Add the carrots and celery which you gently fry for a few minutes.

Add the garlic and give it a good stir before adding the cider and stock – bubble the cider and stock for a few minutes and then add the tomatoes, salt, pepper and sugar.

Simmer this sauce for about 10 minutes before pouring it over the osso buco in the casserole dish. Then add the thyme, cover the dish and cook it in the preheated oven for 2 hours until the meat is soft and delicious.

Mix parsley, garlic and grated zest and sprinkle over just before serving.

Slow-Cooked Oxtail with Five Spice & Ginger

I love this dish and it is very easy to do – some people find it a bit of a fiddle but it is well worth it. Serve with either plain mash or sweet potato mash.

Serves 4

1kg oxtail
1 tablespoon light olive oil
2 medium onions, finely sliced
2½cm fresh ginger, peeled and grated
1 large red chilli, deseeded and chopped
2 garlic cloves, peeled and chopped
1 tablespoon Chinese five spice powder
2 x 400g tins cherry tomatoes
1 litre chicken stock
100ml light soy sauce
75ml light soft brown sugar
1 bunch coriander, leaves separated from stems

Bring the oxtail up to the boil in a large pan of boiling water and simmer for about 20 minutes – drain and rinse. Preheat the oven to 150°C.

Heat the oil in an ovenproof casserole and soften the onions for 10 minutes before adding the grated ginger, chopped chillies and garlic and cook for another few minutes.

Add the chopped stems of the coriander and the five spice powder and cook for a couple of minutes.

Add the tinned tomatoes – cut up the tomatoes with a sharp pair of kitchen scissors as you go. Add the stock and give everything a good stir.

Return the oxtail to the pan and cook very gently on top for 2 hours, or in the oven with a lid on for the 2 hours.

After 2 hours take the oxtail out of the oven or off the stove and add the light soy sauce and brown sugar and cook for another 15 minutes.

Check for salt and pepper and serve with the coriander leaves sprinkled over.

Shona's Bolognese

I think the answer to good bolognese is to cook the mince slowly for a very long time – I make the base of my sauce and then put it in a low oven for about 2 hours or even longer in a casserole dish with a lid. To make sure it does not dry out, put a piece of damp baking paper on top of the mince under the lid – it keeps the moisture in. Also please don't be tempted to buy low fat steak mince, as you need the fat in the beef to make a good bolognese. You can use this as your base for a lasagne or add some chilli flakes or chilli powder and turn it into a chilli con carne, not forgetting to add a tin of kidney beans as well.

Serves 6

1kg good beef mince (I ask the butcher to mince chuck for me)
2 tablespoons light olive oil
2 large onions, finely chopped
1 large carrot, peeled and finely chopped
2 celery sticks, finely chopped
3 garlic cloves, finely chopped
2 glasses white wine or water
2 x 400g tins of tomatoes
2 tablespoons tomato purée
dried (or fresh) oregano or thyme
salt and freshly ground black pepper

Preheat the oven to 140°C.

Warm the olive oil in a heavy casserole dish (one with a lid) and gently fry the onions for 10 minutes until softened.

Add the carrot and celery and fry for another 5 minutes before adding the mince and browning the meat.

Once the meat is all browned add the garlic and give that a good stir for a minute then add the 2 glasses of white wine and bubble away to get all the tasty bits off the bottom of the pan.

Add the tins of tomato, purée and 1 tin of water.

Add a teaspoon of dried oregano or thyme (or fresh leaves if you have them), some salt and pepper and, once bubbling, put in oven for a couple of hours.

Babotie

I really like this dish – it is originally from South Africa but a really good cook friend of mine (Issy Entwisle) gave it to me. I always like her recipes – it's a really good way to use minced lamb.

Serves 6

1 tablespoon vegetable oil
1 onion, finely chopped
2 garlic cloves, finely chopped
1kg lamb mince
2 teaspoons ground coriander
1 teaspoon ground cumin
1 teaspoon paprika
85g fresh breadcrumbs
2 tablespoons white wine vinegar
2 eggs, beaten
4 tablespoons sultanas
4 tablespoons apricot jam or mango chutney
salt and freshly ground black pepper

Topping
2 eggs, beaten
200ml double cream
2 tablespoons fresh coriander or flat-leaf parsley, chopped

Preheat the oven to 170°C.

Line a 26cm loose-bottomed cake tin with non-stick baking paper.

Heat the oil in frying pan and fry the onion gently for 10 minutes and then add the garlic for a few minutes.

Add the spices and cook for another few minutes.

Add the meat and fry and stir until browned. Add the white wine vinegar.

Take off the heat and mix in the breadcrumbs, beaten eggs, sultanas, apricot jam, and salt and pepper to taste.

Turn the mixture into the prepared tin and spread evenly.

For the topping – beat the eggs and cream in a bowl together and season well – pour over the meat and scatter over the coriander.

Put the tin on a baking sheet and bake for 1 hour.

Serve with yoghurt and pitta bread.

Lamb & Vegetable Stew

This is such an easy dish to make – you can make it with the lamb as below or leave the lamb out altogether and you have a wonderful vegetable stew. It is good served with rice or bulgur.

Serves 4

500g neck fillet of lamb, cubed
10 baby onions, peeled and sliced
8 garlic cloves, peeled and sliced
450g sweet potatoes or ordinary potatoes, peeled and cut into chunks
4 red peppers, deseeded and sliced
500g aubergines, cut into chunks
900g tomatoes, cut into chunks
½ teaspoon of ground black pepper
1½ teaspoons salt
2 tablespoons light olive oil

Preheat the oven to 170°C.

Spread the lamb over the base of an ovenproof dish.

Spread the onions on top and the garlic – next the potatoes – then the aubergines – then the peppers – then the tomatoes.

Drizzle over oil. Add ground black pepper and 1½ teaspoons of sea salt.

Put on a lid and cook in the oven for 2 hours.

Pot Roasted Brisket of Beef with Red Wine & Thyme

I think my sister, Nicky, gave me this recipe. She has given me so many slow-cooked recipes over the years, as she has an Aga. She leaves things in the slow oven for hours. It is another dish of the sort of food I love – slow-cooked yummy beef with a rich sauce of winter vegetables with thyme.

Preheat the oven to 150°C.

Find a casserole dish which will fit the brisket in with the vegetables – one that has a lid.

Peel the vegetables and cut the parsnips, carrots and turnips into chunks.

Peel the onions and slice them, and cut the celery into thin slices.

Put 1 tablespoon of oil in the casserole dish and brown the brisket on all sides and remove.

Add another tablespoon of oil and gently fry the onions until soft for 10 minutes and then add the other vegetables.

Put the meat back in the pan.

In another saucepan reduce the red wine with the thyme, orange peel,

Serves 6

1.2kg brisket of beef
2 parsnips
4 carrots
2 onions
2 celery sticks
2 small turnips
2 tablespoons light olive oil
1 bunch flat-leaf parsley, coarsely chopped
3 sprigs fresh thyme
750ml red wine
2 tablespoons redcurrant jelly
1 bay leaf
peel of ¼ orange

redcurrant jelly and bay leaf until it is reduced by half, and then pour on top of the beef.

Add the flat-leaf parsley, salt and pepper.

Cover with a sheet of greaseproof paper and put the lid on the casserole and roast in the oven for 2½ to 3 hours – take it out to check it is nicely slow-cooked and soft if you put a knife in. I would check after 2 hours and if the wine is reduced too much and things look a bit dry, add about 500ml of chicken stock if you have it, or water will do.

My Cottage Pie

This is another recipe for JoJo Palmer, for whose large extended family I have cooked for years and years – weddings, birthday parties and now her grandchildren's christenings. However many different menus I send her, she always wants one of my lasagnas or cottage pies! Probably everyone has their own recipe for shepherds' pie or cottage pie but I could not write this book without putting this in just for my friends who really hardly cook and would like this recipe! Many people have asked me to. As with the lasagne recipe, I would urge you to buy good mince for this recipe and not the lean mince from supermarkets labelled 'steak mince', as there is just not enough fat on it to make the meat tasty enough.

Serves 4–6

1kg chuck beef mince
40g butter
2 onions, finely chopped
2 carrots, finely chopped
1 tablespoon plain flour
500ml chicken stock or water
1 tablespoon Lea & Perrins Worcestershire sauce
1 tablespoon tomato ketchup

Mash
1kg Maris Piper potatoes or King Edwards, peeled and cut into equal chunks
60g butter, melted and warm
4 tablespoons single cream or full-fat milk, warmed
salt and freshly ground black pepper

Start by gently frying the onions for 10 minutes until very soft in the butter, then add the finely chopped carrots.

Add the beef mince and brown all over by giving it a good stir from time to time. Once the meat is brown stir in the plain flour, then add the chicken stock, Worcester sauce and tomato ketchup.

Season to taste.

Stir the mixture up well – you may need to add some more water. At this point leave it to bubble very low for a couple of hours, stirring regularly. Once ready you can start making the mashed potatoes. Put the meat mixture in an appropriately sized ovenproof dish.

Beef & Lamb

Preheat the oven to 170°C.

Boil the potatoes in a pan of boiling salted water for 20 minutes (I always use a timer) and then drain really well – wet potatoes make horrible mash.

I then break the potatoes up with a fork and mash a bit before adding the warm butter and cream or milk. I actually use an electric hand whisk and give a good old beating until the potatoes are soft and creamy.

Check for seasoning and then spread on top of the mince and cook in the preheated oven for 25 minutes.

Lamb, Sweet Potato & Orzo Stew

Another delicious slow-cooked, soft lamb dish which I love. Great served on its own with some chopped parsley and a dollop of fresh thick yoghurt, and maybe a flatbread or two.

Serves 4

3 tablespoons vegetable oil
2 onions, finely chopped
2 cinnamon sticks
½ teaspoon chilli flakes
½ teaspoon dried oregano
2 sprigs thyme
salt and freshly ground black pepper
1kg lamb neck fillet, cut into chunks
1 x 400g tin of cherry tomatoes
900ml fresh chicken stock
400g sweet potatoes, peeled and cut into 4cm cubes
200g orzo

Preheat the oven to 150°C.

Put the oil into a casserole dish which has a lid.

Fry the onions for a good 10 minutes gently until they are soft.

Add the cinnamon sticks, chilli flakes, oregano, thyme and salt and pepper and stir for a few minutes until the herbs are integrated with the onions and you have a wonderful smell coming from the casserole.

Add the lamb to the pot – a small bit at a time – giving a good stir so it all gets slightly browned and covered in the spice mixture.

Once all browned, add the stock and tomatoes – keep stirring for a few minutes and then cover the top with some Bakewell paper and then the lid and put in the preheated oven for 1.5 hours.

Take out of the oven and add the sweet potato and return to the oven for 20 minutes.

Take the pot out of the oven once again and add the orzo and put back in the oven for another 20 minutes.

Chateaubriand with Béarnaise

A chateaubriand steak is cut from the thickest part of a trimmed fillet – it should weigh about 350g, enough for two people. When I was a little girl in Jersey this was my absolute treat when going out to a restaurant – but I had to persuade another member of the family to share as it was always done for two. It is horribly expensive at a restaurant these days and probably was all those years ago too – my poor long-suffering father always paid then. Always take your meat out of the fridge and bring it to room temperature before cooking it – that is such an important factor and often recipes omit this detail.

Serves 2

350g centre cut fillet of beef
1 tablespoon light olive oil
freshly ground black pepper

Cheat's Béarnaise sauce
Serves 2–6

250g butter
6 tablespoons white wine vinegar
2 tablespoons fresh tarragon, chopped
5 egg yolks

Preheat the oven to 200°C.

Paint your room-temperature beef with the light olive oil and sprinkle with pepper.

Heat an ovenproof griddle pan on the top of your stove until piping hot – hold your hand above the pan to check – then pop the fillet in the pan and with tongs give it a minute on either side until nicely browned all over.

Put the pan in the hot oven for 12 minutes, then take out of oven and leave to rest for 5 minutes and cut into thick slices to serve.

Cheat's Béarnaise sauce

This is very easy but you definitely need room-temperature eggs before you start. This will make more than you need for 2 people – probably enough for 6

– but I have found if you try to make it in smaller amounts, for some scientific reason it does not work for me.

Put the egg yolks into the bowl of a food processor.

Put the white wine vinegar into a small heavy-based saucepan and boil away until you have 1 tablespoon reduced vinegar left. You really have to watch this – the times I have boiled away the whole lot and been left with our whole house smelling of vinegar!

Melt the butter over a gentle flame until the whole lot is bubbling – then switch on the motor of the food processor and mix the eggs well – very gently pour on the really hot butter which in itself cooks the eggs.

Add the reduced vinegar and tip out of the food processor into a bowl for serving.

Add the tarragon and taste for salt and pepper.

Tip It will keep in the fridge for days and days – all you need to do is bring it to room temperature and it will soften ready for your use. If you want to hurry the softening process, put it over a bowl of hot water and give it a good stir.

Beef & Lamb

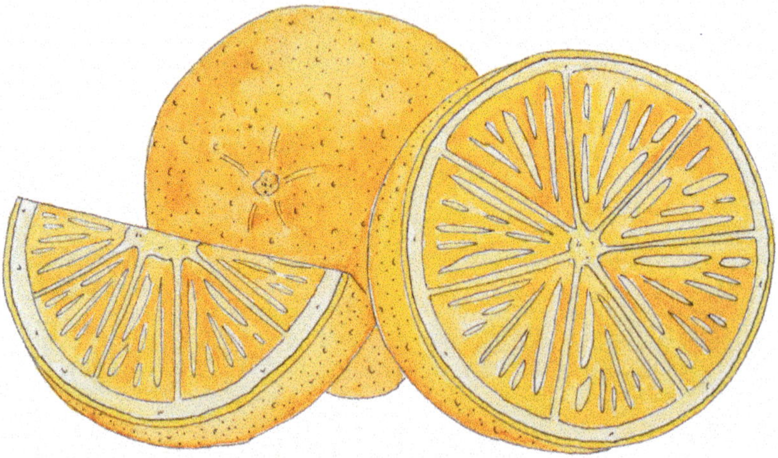

Game, Duck & Guinea Fowl

Braised Duck with Orange, Port & Dried Cherries

This is a really good slow-cooked duck recipe – the end result is the meat just falling off the bone. Serve with a creamy mash and shredded cabbage, lightly sautéed.

Serves 6

6 duck legs
1 onion, finely sliced
75g cubed pancetta
150ml port
425ml fresh chicken stock or water
1 teaspoon tomato purée
1 orange
1 bay leaf
3 sprigs thyme
salt and freshly ground black pepper
25g dried cherries or cranberries
1 tablespoon redcurrant jelly

Preheat the oven to 100°C.

Warm a large frying pan and brown the duck legs slowly (there is enough fat in the duck so don't add any oil).

Remove to a plate and tip off the excess fat.

Add the onion and cook gently for about 10 minutes until beginning to soften.

Add the pancetta and cook for a further 3–4 minutes.

Pour in the port, bring to the boil, bubble for a minute and then add the stock and tomato purée.

Grate the zest from half the orange and add to the liquid along with the bay leaf, thyme, seasoning and cranberries or dried cherries.

Return the duck to the pan and baste with the sauce.

Cover and cook in oven for 3 hours.

Lift the duck from the sauce on to a serving dish and skim off any excess fat.

Remove the thyme and bay leaf, add the redcurrant jelly and bubble up the sauce on top of the stove until slightly reduced.

Country Pheasant Casserole

Another wonderful recipe from my old friend, Chesty (Helen Mullens), who is an excellent cook and always gives me lovely recipes. She lives in the middle of the country and always seems to have a brace of pheasant in her freezer! All you need is a delicious baked potato to go with it or lovely creamy mash.

Serves 4

- 2 tablespoons rapeseed oil or vegetable oil
- 30g butter
- 2 pheasants
- 125g streaky bacon
- 30g plain flour
- 250ml red wine
- 250ml good stock
- 2 tablespoons redcurrant jelly or bramble jelly
- 1 tablespoon fresh thyme
- salt and freshly ground black pepper
- 16 shallot onions

Preheat oven to 120°C.

Heat the butter and oil in a large pan and brown the pheasants.

Remove from the pan – then fry the bacon and remove.

Stir the flour into the fat and cook for a minute.

Gradually stir in the wine and stock – bring to the boil and thicken.

Add the fruit jelly, thyme and onions and return the bacon and pheasant to the pan and cook for 4 hours.

Once cooked, remove the birds from the pan, cool and take all the meat off the bone and add to the sauce.

Duck Breasts with Pomegranate Molasses

This is very quick to do. I actually prefer the slow-cooked duck leg recipes, but many people prefer pink duck breasts, so I have put this recipe in my collection and hope you enjoy it. We have done this for several weddings for large numbers and it has worked well. It reminds me of a wonderful South African au pair we had staying with us, Carise Horn, who ended up going back to Cape Town and setting up her own very successful catering company. She gave me this recipe.

Serves 4

4 duck breasts with their skin on
1 tablespoon light olive oil or vegetable oil
2 tablespoons water
2 tablespoons pomegranate molasses
pinch ground cinnamon
sea salt and freshly ground black pepper

Preheat the oven to 200°C.

Score the skin of the breasts well in a criss-cross way, salt and leave for 15 minutes.

Place a good heavy frying pan with a heat resistant handle (i.e. one that can go in the oven) over a medium heat.

When hot, put the breasts in skin side down and seal slowly until well browned. Then turn over and brown the flesh sides of the birds.

Place the pan in the oven for 15 minutes.

Take out of the oven and rest on a board and put the pan back on the heat.

Add 1 tablespoon of light olive oil to the pan with the pomegranate molasses, water and cinnamon and give it a good old stir to scrape all the bits off the bottom of the pan into the juices.

Reduce for a minute and add salt and pepper.

Slice each breast into 3 or 4 pieces at an angle and pour the sauce over.

Guinea Fowl with Grapes & Port

This is another good guinea fowl recipe – I had it at a friend's house in the country years ago and then again recently, so here it is. Wonderful in the winter with creamy mash and cabbage.

Serves 2–3 – depending on how greedy you are!

1 guinea fowl
1 tablespoon olive oil
15g butter
1 onion
2 garlic cloves
100g black or red grapes
200ml port
50ml chicken stock
1 bay leaf
30g blanched hazelnuts
100g raisins
150ml cold tea
1 tablespoon parsley, roughly chopped

Preheat the oven to 180°C.

Melt butter and oil in a small casserole dish with a heavy base. Brown the guinea fowl and remove.

Add the chopped onion and cook over a low heat for 10 minutes until soft.

Add the garlic and cook for another minute. Turn off the heat.

Put the raisins and tea into a small saucepan and bring to the boil – turn off the heat and leave to soak for 30 minutes.

Toast the hazelnuts and then crush them.

Put the guinea fowl back into the casserole and add the raisins, tea, grapes, nuts, port, chicken stock and bay leaf.

Bring to the boil and then cover the pot firmly and put into the oven for 45 minutes.

Remove the lid and cook for another 15 minutes.

When the cooking time has finished, if the sauce looks too thin, take the bird out and boil the sauce for a bit longer to thicken it.

Stir in the parsley and serve.

Guinea Fowl with Peas & Pancetta

Another lovely casserole dish – great for autumn. You could also make it with chicken supremes with skin on or even chicken thighs with skin and bone. Lovely with mashed potato.

Serves 6

6 guinea fowl breasts with skin on
4 tablespoons flour
4 tablespoons olive oil
12 baby onions or shallots, peeled
130g pancetta cubes
2 leeks, trimmed and sliced
2 garlic cloves, crushed
250ml dry white wine
510ml chicken stock
1 bay leaf
250g frozen peas, thawed
2 tablespoons flat-leaf parsley, chopped
salt and freshly ground black pepper

Preheat the oven to 180°C.

Dust the guinea fowl breasts lightly with flour. Heat half the oil in a large frying pan and cook in batches, adding oil if needed, until browned. Transfer to a large casserole dish.

Heat the remaining oil in the pan over a moderate heat.

Add the onions or shallots, and cook stirring occasionally for 5 minutes or until lightly golden. Remove to the casserole.

Add the pancetta, leeks and garlic to the pan and cook, stirring occasionally for 7–10 minutes, or until tender. Add to the casserole.

Stir the wine, stock and bay leaf into the casserole and bring to the boil. Cover, transfer to the oven and cook for 1 hour, stirring occasionally.

Stir in the peas and cook for a further 15 minutes.

Remove the guinea fowl and keep warm.

Reduce the liquid over a high heat for 5–10 minutes, or until it reaches sauce consistency.

Remove the bay leaf, stir in the parsley and season to taste.

Slow-Cooked Duck Legs with Soy, Ginger & Star Anise

This is completely delicious and I love the slow-cooked texture of the duck meat – it is lovely served with parsnip purée and some wilted spinach.

Serves 4

4 duck legs
3 garlic cloves, sliced
3cm fresh ginger, cut into matchsticks
2 star anise
2½ tablespoons of Sake
250ml chicken stock
75ml light soy sauce
½ teaspoon five spice powder
2 tablespoons runny honey

Preheat the oven to 150°C.

Heat a large frying pan over a low heat.

Add the duck legs with no extra fat and cook until brown on both sides, which will take about 20 minutes.

Transfer the duck legs to a baking pan. Pour away the duck fat.

Put the pan back on the heat, add ginger and garlic and cook for a couple of minutes.

Add the star anise, Sake, stock and soy and let it bubble for 5 minutes.

Pour this over the duck legs and add the honey and five spice powder.

Wrap the pan in foil, sealing the pan well and bake for an hour.

Remove the pan from the oven, take off the foil.

Turn the oven up to 200°C and roast the duck for a further 15 minutes.

Venison Stew with Redcurrant Jelly & Red Wine

This is a lovely winter recipe we have served at weddings for people who love a rustic, hearty dish. You can also make it with chuck steak cut into chunks – but cook the beef for 3 hours instead of 2.

Preheat the oven to 150°C.

Fry the vegetables in a little oil and butter in a heavy-based casserole dish for 4–5 minutes until golden.

Tip in the garlic and fry for a further minute, then set aside.

Put the venison into a plastic bag with seasoned flour and shake to coat.

Add a little more oil and butter to the pan, then fry the venison over a high heat, stirring now and then, until well browned. Don't crowd the pan – cook in batches if necessary.

Set aside with the vegetables.

Add the redcurrant jelly and wine to the pan, and bring to the boil, scraping up all the bits that have stuck to the bottom.

Serves 8

2 carrots, roughly chopped
140g turnips or swede, roughly chopped
2 onions, roughly chopped
3 celery sticks, roughly chopped
Light olive oil and butter for frying
1 garlic clove, crushed
1kg boned leg or shoulder of venison, cut into large chunks, or buy ready-cubed venison for stewing
5 tablespoons plain flour, seasoned with salt and freshly ground black pepper
2 tablespoons redcurrant jelly or rowan jelly or hawthorn jelly
450ml dry red wine
450ml beef stock
2 sprigs thyme
1 bay leaf

Pour in the stock, then add the thyme, bay leaf, meat and vegetables. Season if you like and bring to the boil.

Cover and transfer to the oven for about 2 hours or until tender.

Remove from the oven and check the seasoning.

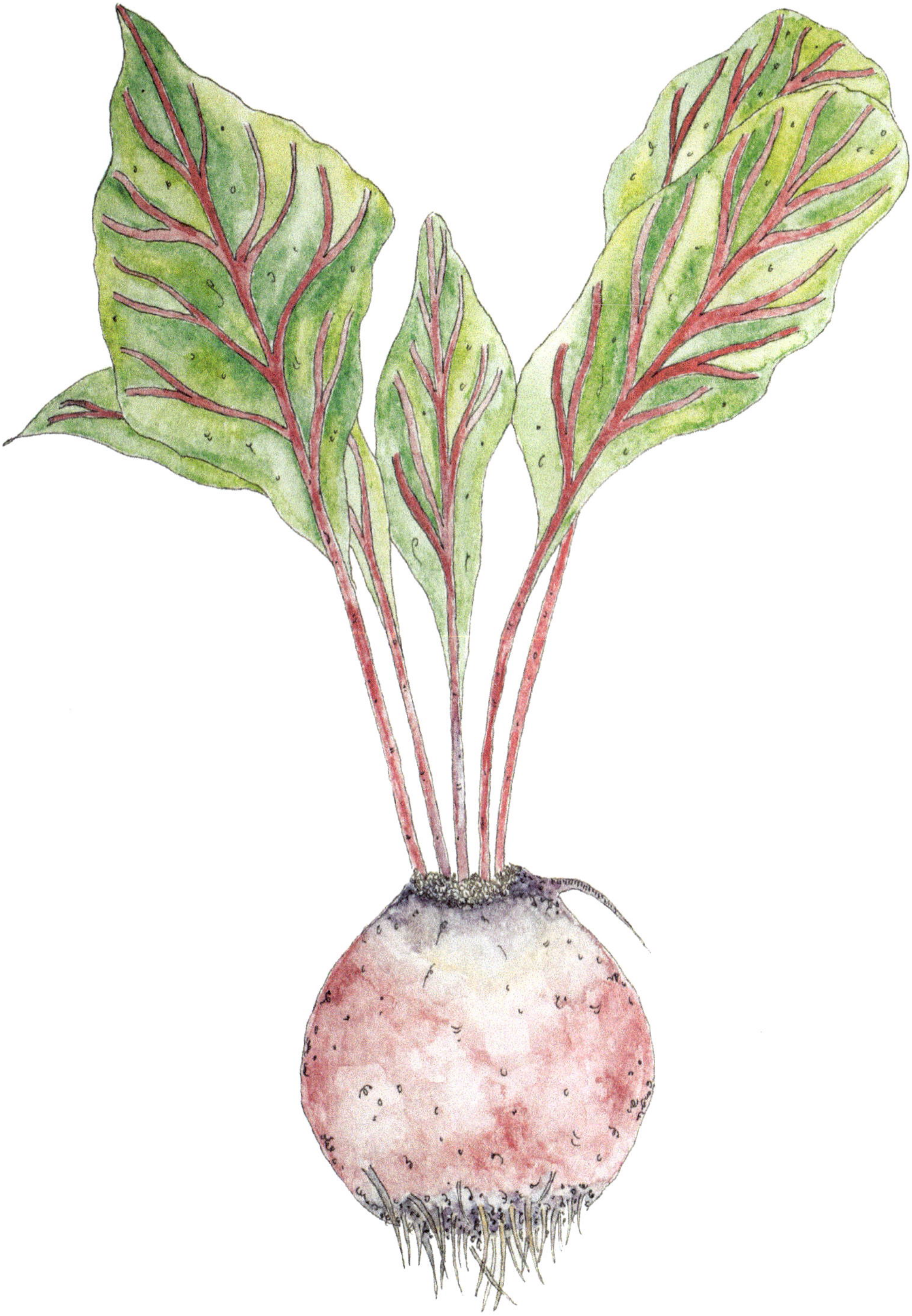

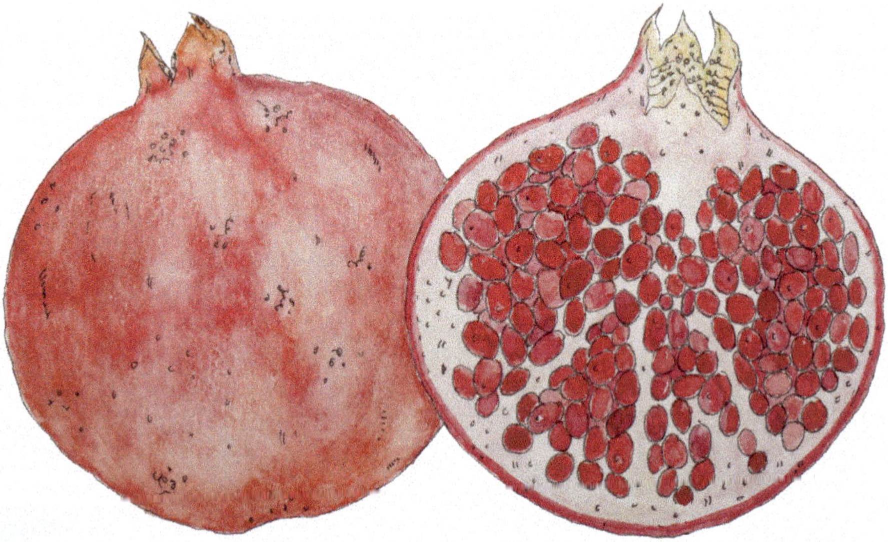

Sauces

Bridget Jackson's Mustard Sauce (for Ham)

This is a delicious, simple recipe – serve it with roast gammon either hot or cold. It is like a thick vinaigrette and lovely with any cold meats.

Makes one small jam jar

2 tablespoons Dijon mustard
1 tablespoon wine vinegar
1 tablespoon sugar
½ teaspoon freshly ground black pepper
6 tablespoons light olive oil

Mix the first four ingredients and slowly whisk in the oil until the sauce thickens and is a mayonnaise consistency.

Chilli Jam

I do this when I find I have a surplus of tomatoes and it keeps for ages in the fridge. It is a delicious addition to a cheeseboard or mixed with cream cheese to make a zingy dip.

Makes about 6 jars

500g very ripe tomatoes
4 garlic cloves, peeled
4 large red chillies (seeds left in if you want your jam hot)
5cm piece of fresh ginger, sliced
300g golden caster sugar
2 tablespoons Thai fish sauce
100ml red wine vinegar

Blitz half the tomatoes with all the garlic, chillies and ginger in a food processor.

Pour into a heavy-based saucepan.

Add the sugar, fish sauce and vinegar, and bring to the boil.

Dice the remaining tomatoes finely and add them to the pan.

Simmer for 30–40 minutes, stirring from time to time. The mixture will turn slightly darker and sticky.

Store in warm dry sterilised jars and seal while the mixture is still warm.

Tip The longer you keep this jam the hotter it gets. It keeps for about 3 months in the fridge.

Nan's Green Tomato Chutney

This recipe is from my wonderful Auntie Nan (my father's sister) – I always think of her whilst I am making it. Again, probably only of interest to my family for pure nostalgia!

Makes enough for 6 medium-sized jam jars

2kg green tomatoes (red will do if you can't find green)
2kg green apples
2kg shallots, peeled and coarsely minced in a blender
1kg demerara sugar
1 litre vinegar
500g sultanas
75g peeled and sliced fresh ginger
3 red chillies, deseeded and chopped
75g salt

Dissolve sugar in the vinegar.

Mix everything together and boil slowly until the sauce thickens and starts to set like jam.

Red Onion Marmalade

This is a recipe I was given by the owner of the 'Dining Room Shop' in Barnes. Sadly, it closed a few years ago but I cooked it for them one year to sell in their shop and held onto the recipe – it really works.

Chop the onions finely. Sprinkle on salt and leave for 2 hours. Rinse and dry.

Put the sugar, vinegar and cloves to boil and then simmer for 5 minutes.

Add onions and caraway seeds and return to boil, then simmer for two and a half hours until thick and set.

Put mixture into sterilised jam jars and keep.

Makes enough for 4 medium-sized jam jars

1kg preserving sugar
1kg red onions
500ml vinegar
2 tablespoons salt
2 teaspoons caraway seeds
1½ teaspoons cloves, ground

Salad Dressings

So often salads are ruined by over-strong dressings. More and more I just put a tablespoon of really good cider vinegar at the bottom of the salad bowl, add 3 tablespoons of light olive oil and give it a good stir – add a good pinch of salt and freshly ground black pepper. Give it all a good toss…

Vinaigrette

Makes a lot – keeps for a few days in a nice Kilner jar or old jam jar.

Makes about 350ml

- pinch of caster sugar
- salt and freshly ground black pepper
- 2 tablespoons of red wine vinegar
- 2 tablespoons of Dijon mustard
- 4 tablespoons of tepid tap water
- 120ml of sunflower oil/ any flavourless oil
- 120ml of extra-virgin olive oil

Put sugar, salt, pepper, vinegar and mustard in a blender. Add water and blend together.

With the motor running, pour in the oils, one after the other in a thin stream until thick and homogenised – you are aiming for the consistency of pouring cream – if too thick add some water.

Balsamic Dressing

This is a good dressing which I make a lot.

Makes about 350ml

- 1 large garlic clove
- 1 level teaspoon sea salt
- 1 teaspoon powdered English mustard
- 2 tablespoons of balsamic vinegar
- 2 tablespoons of walnut oil
- 3 tablespoons light olive oil

Use a pestle and mortar to pound the garlic with the salt until it's creamy then add the mustard and mix well.

After that whisk in the balsamic vinegar followed by the oils, then season well with salt and freshly ground black pepper.

Wiz's Simple Dressing

This is excellent too.

Put all ingredients in a jam jar and shake well.

1 tablespoon white wine vinegar
1 teaspoon caster sugar
good pinch of salt
freshly ground black pepper
1 tablespoon extra-virgin olive oil
2 tablespoons flavourless oil

My Stepmother Ann's Dressing

We always had this as children at home at our lovely house, right by the sea in Jersey.

Put the mustard, honey, garlic and red wine vinegar in a salad bowl and whisk until well combined.

Continue whisking and slowly add the olive oil to make a thick and creamy dressing.

Add salt and freshly ground black pepper to taste.

1 tablespoon Dijon mustard
1 tablespoon runny honey
1 garlic clove, crushed
2 tablespoons red wine vinegar
6 tablespoons light olive oil
salt and freshly ground black pepper

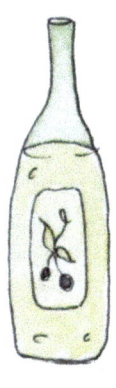

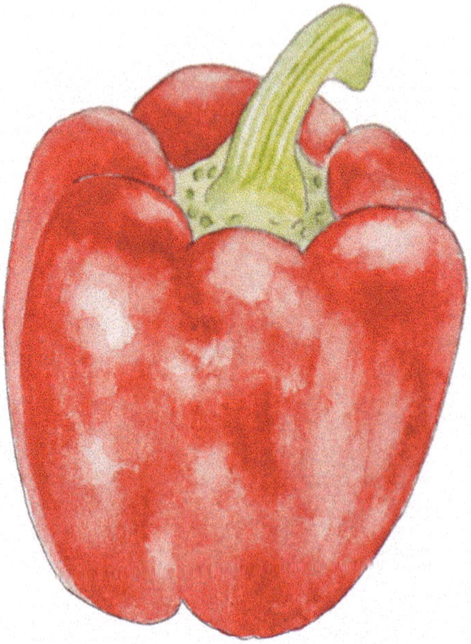

Vegetarian

Many of these vegetarian recipes can be quickly adapted to be vegan, by simply exchanging butter for olive oil or vegan margarine, and there are plenty of vegan cheese alternatives available.

Aubergine Parmigiana

This recipe is for the Snow family – some of my most loyal clients. I have been cooking for Peter and Ann during lockdown and this is her absolute favourite. Quite rich, and most important is the really good tomato sauce: once made it's a base for any tomato pasta sauce, or add to Mediterranean vegetables for ratatouille or briam.

Serves 4

Tomato sauce
- 2–3 tablespoons light olive oil
- 2 onions, finely chopped
- 2 garlic cloves, finely chopped
- 2 celery sticks, finely chopped
- 1 large carrot, peeled and finely chopped
- 1 tsp light soft brown sugar
- a few sprigs of fresh thyme
- 3 x 400g tins good plum tomatoes or passata
- 2 tablespoons tomato purée
- salt and black pepper

The parmigiana
- 2 very large aubergines
- 2 tablespoons light olive oil
- 2 balls mozzarella, thinly sliced
- 2 tablespoons grated Parmesan

Gently fry the onions in the light olive oil for 10 minutes until soft, then add the chopped carrots and celery and cook gently for another few minutes.

Add the chopped garlic, the tins of tomatoes or passata and the tomato purée.

Add the sugar, salt and pepper and leaves from the sprigs of thyme.

Preheat the oven to 200°C.

Line a large baking tray with greaseproof paper.

Cut the aubergine lengthways and then in chunky slices. Put in a mixing bowl with the light olive oil and some salt and give a good stir with your hands.

Bake in oven for about 35–40 minutes until the aubergines are well browned.

Get a nice ovenproof dish ready – cover the base with some tomato sauce – then a layer of aubergines then a layer of mozzarella. Continue layering, finishing with a layer of mozzarella and a sprinkling of grated Parmesan.

Bake in the hot oven for 30 minutes until it is bubbling at the edges.

Blue Cheese & Spinach Tart with Caramelised Onions

This is a delicious tart and you could change the blue cheese for Gruyère should you prefer, or cheddar if you don't have Gruyère. It freezes very well.

Make the pastry case: melt butter in pan and then stir in plain flour and add the water. Push pastry into tart tin and leave in fridge for 10 minutes to cool.

Preheat the oven to 170°C.

When oven is hot, bake the pastry blind for 15 minutes or until the pastry is golden.

Make the filling – melt the butter in a non-stick frying pan over a low heat, stir in the onions and gently fry until very soft but not brown, sprinkle with salt and sugar and cook for a few minutes more, stirring occasionally until deep golden brown.

Prepare the spinach by stripping the leaves off their stalks and then rolling them up and slicing them into thin strips.

Serves 6

4 onions, finely sliced
90g butter
1 tablespoon light soft brown sugar
salt and freshly ground black pepper
125g ready-washed spinach leaves
175g blue cheese (or any other cheese if you don't like blue)
6 tablespoons mascarpone cheese
2 tablespoons double cream or crème fraîche
5 eggs

Pastry case
300g butter
500g plain flour
1 pudding spoon water

Mix the mascarpone with the blue cheese, egg and double cream or crème fraîche.

Assemble the tart by putting the onions in the pastry case, then the spinach and the mascarpone mixture on top – using a spatula to spread.

Bake the tart until the topping is puffed and golden, for about 20 minutes, until firm to touch. Serve warm with a lovely simple salad.

Vicky's Courgette Pasta Dish

I have tried so hard to find interesting vegetarian dishes and this one is really good. My friend, Vicky Spendlove, gave it to us when she hosted lunch for us chalet girls who worked in Méribel in 1975/76. This is wonderful served with a lovely light mixed leaf salad and some good bread (and butter of course).

Serves 6

- 6 small to medium courgettes, thinly sliced
- salt and freshly ground black pepper
- 1 onion, finely chopped
- 2 garlic cloves, finely chopped
- 30g butter
- 2 tablespoons light olive oil
- 150ml sour cream or crème fraîche
- 1 small bunch dill, finely chopped
- 300g pasta of your choice
- 3 tablespoons finely grated Parmesan

Melt the butter and oil in a heavy, wide pan and gently fry the onion for 10 minutes until very soft – then add the garlic for a minute.

Give a good stir and then add the sliced courgettes and cook for another 5 minutes until the courgettes have softened.

Add the cream and salt and freshly ground black pepper and bubble it all up for a few minutes.

Turn off the heat and add the chopped dill – check to see if seasoning is to your taste.

In the meantime, you will have cooked the pasta according to the instructions on the pack – usually bring a large pan of water up to the boil with a pinch of salt and then throw in the 300g pasta. Bring back to the boil and cook for 10 minutes.

Serve the pasta with the sauce in bowls with grated Parmesan.

Veggie Shepherd's Pie with Sweet Potato Mash

A delicious vegetarian shepherd's pie – a really lovely alternative to the meaty version.

Serves 4

1 tablespoon vegetable oil
1 large onion, halved and sliced
500g carrots, cut into small pieces
2 tablespoons thyme, chopped
200ml red wine
1 x 400g tin chopped tomatoes
½ teaspoon salt
410g tin cooked Puy lentils
950g sweet potatoes, peeled and cut into small chunks
25g butter
85g vegetarian mature cheddar, grated

Preheat the oven to 180°C.

Heat the oil in a frying pan, then fry the onion slices gently until soft and golden.

Add the carrots and most of the thyme.

Pour in the wine, 150ml water, tomatoes and salt and simmer for 10 minutes.

Tip in the tin of lentils, including their juice, then cover and simmer for another 10 minutes until the carrots still have a bit of bite and the lentils are pulpy.

Meanwhile, boil the sweet potatoes for 15 minutes until tender, drain well, then mash with the butter and season to taste.

Pile the lentil mixture into a pie dish, spoon the mash on top, then sprinkle over the cheese and remaining thyme.

Cook for 20 minutes if cooking straight away, or for 40 minutes from chilled, until golden and hot all the way through. Serve with broccoli.

Tip The uncooked pie can be covered and chilled for 2 days, or frozen for up to a month.

Mushroom Risotto

This is another recipe from my old cookery school – gosh the recipes there were all good and they worked. I always use this when asked to do a vegetarian risotto for a client – it is wonderful. If it must be strictly vegetarian, use vegetarian stock, but I think it is nicer with really good chicken stock.

Serves 4

1 large onion, finely chopped
1 garlic clove, finely chopped
90g butter
350g Italian risotto rice
1 litre homemade chicken stock or vegetable stock, heated
350g chestnut mushrooms, sliced
salt and freshly ground black pepper
110g Parmesan, grated

Fry the sliced mushrooms in 45g of the butter until soft and set aside.

Melt the other 45g of the butter and cook the onion for a good 10 minutes until beautifully soft. Add the finely chopped garlic and cook for another minute or two – don't whatever you do let the garlic burn.

In with the rice and stir until the grains are nice and buttery.

Heat the stock and add it a tablespoon at a time – only adding more as each tablespoon is absorbed. After about 25 minutes the rice should be creamy and soft but not like porridge.

Season to taste.

Add the sliced mushrooms and give a good old stir and then 25g of the Parmesan.

When serving, pass the rest of the Parmesan around the table for people to add to their yummy dish.

Puy Lentil & Pecan Stew with Sweet Potatoes & Feta

This is a lovely vegetarian dish we have served at many weddings. You can leave out the feta if you don't like feta, or if you would like it to be vegan. It is wholesome and very good.

Serves 4

3 tablespoons light olive oil
1 medium onion, finely chopped
1 carrot, finely chopped
1 celery stick, finely chopped
2 garlic cloves, finely chopped
2 fresh bay leaves
125g chestnut mushrooms
300g sweet potatoes
200g Puy lentils
700ml chicken or vegetable stock
80g pecans
100g feta
2 tablespoons flat-leaf parsley, chopped

Preheat the oven to 180°C.

Peel and cut the sweet potato into wedges. Mix with 1 tablespoon light olive oil and salt and put into preheated oven for 25 minutes or until cooked through.

Melt the other 2 tablespoons olive oil in heavy-based casserole dish (one with a lid preferably) and soften the onion for 10 minutes before adding the garlic, carrot and celery.

Add the mushrooms and fry for another 5 minutes or until mushrooms are soft.

Now add the lentils and stock and bubble for about 30 minutes.

When the lentils are cooked add the sweet potato and pecans.

Check for seasoning and add salt and pepper if necessary. Just before serving, sprinkle on the feta and parsley. Yum.

Spinach & Feta Tart

We do this often for vegetarians either as part of a cold summer buffet or warm in the winter at a wedding. It is very easy, especially if you have some frozen leaf spinach in your freezer.

Serves 8

Pastry
150g butter, melted
240g plain flour
½ teaspoon salt
1 tablespoon cold water

Filling
450g frozen leaf spinach, defrosted and drained
170g feta, crumbled
freshly grated nutmeg
freshly ground black pepper
½ teaspoon salt
4 whole eggs, beaten
300ml double or single cream

I use my push-in pastry for this tart – here is the recipe again.

Preheat the oven to 180°C.

Melt the butter in a pan and stir in the flour and salt – stir it around to make a pastry paste and then add the cold water.

Just push this into a 24cm loose-bottomed tart tin – as thinly as you can – and then bake for 20 minutes in the preheated oven until golden brown. Let it cool.

Drain the frozen spinach really well and when the pastry is cool spread the spinach around the base – crumble over the feta.

Beat the eggs well with the cream – add the nutmeg, salt and pepper and pour over the spinach and feta.

Bake in oven for 25 minutes until well browned. Either eat straight away or let it cool and freeze, or keep in the fridge until you want to eat it.

Spinach & Ricotta Lasagne

This has proved very popular during the Covid lockdown and so I thought I should include it. Thanks to my loyal lockdown delivery clients, I have served this most weeks. You could add blue cheese to the sauce if you like it, but I make it with just ricotta and Parmesan.

Serves 6

Spinach and cheese mixture
450g frozen spinach, defrosted and really well drained
225g ricotta
50g Parmesan, grated
1 teaspoon freshly grated nutmeg
1 tablespoon roasted pine nuts
about 8–10 dried lasagne sheets

Sauce
60g butter, melted
60g plain flour
700ml full-fat milk
salt and freshly ground pepper

Preheat the oven to 180°C.

First make the sauce by melting the butter and stirring in the flour over a low flame.

Add the milk slowly and stir constantly until the sauce is bubbling.

Take off the heat and add the nutmeg, salt and pepper.

Add the spinach, ricotta and Parmesan.

Add the roasted pine nuts.

Put a third of the sauce in a medium-sized ovenproof pie dish and cover with lasagne sheets. Put another third of the sauce on top, then cover again with lasagne sheets. Finally, put the remaining sauce on top and cover with the grated Parmesan.

Bake in oven for about 30 minutes until browned and bubbling.

Butternut Squash & Coconut Curry with Cashew Nuts

We often serve this as a vegetarian option at a wedding and it can also be gluten-free. You can get Thai basil from a Thai supermarket – if not just use normal basil. Sometimes we have stirred in some fresh spinach leaves just before serving and if you would like to make it more substantial you can add a tin of chickpeas.

Serves 8

2 onions, finely chopped
2 tablespoons rapeseed oil or sunflower oil
3 garlic cloves, finely chopped
4 spring onions, finely sliced
zest and juice of 2 limes
1 teaspoon ground coriander
2 teaspoons ground cumin
3cm fresh ginger, peeled and coarsely grated
2 red chillies, deseeded and finely chopped
1 tablespoon light soy sauce
1 small bunch Thai basil, torn
1 small bunch coriander, chopped
1 tablespoon peanut butter
2 x 400ml tins of coconut milk
2kg butternut squash, peeled and chopped into chunks
2 tablespoons toasted cashew nuts

Gently fry onions in the rapeseed or sunflower oil until soft – about 10 minutes.

Add the spring onions and fry for a few more minutes.

Add the ground coriander, cumin, ginger, red chillies and give it a good stir for a few minutes.

Now you can add the lime zest and juice and the garlic, the soy sauce and peanut butter. Give another stir and add the coconut milk and the butternut squash and cook on top slowly for about 30 minutes.

Just before serving add the cashew nuts, coriander and basil.

Vegetarian Goulash

A lovely vegetarian dish – serve either with flatbreads or rice and top with a dollop of thick yoghurt. You could even put some finely chopped avocado and chopped cherry tomatoes on top of the yoghurt.

Serves 4–6

2 tablespoons light olive oil
2 medium onions, chopped
1 tablespoon flour
1 tablespoon paprika
pinch cayenne pepper
1 x 400g tin of tomatoes
275ml boiling water
1 teaspoon tomato purée
225g cauliflower divided into florets
225g carrots, chopped
225g new potatoes, in half
2 red peppers, deseeded and sliced
150ml thick yoghurt
salt and freshly ground black pepper

Preheat the oven to 170°C.

Fry the onions in the olive oil in an ovenproof casserole for 10 minutes until softened.

Add the flour, paprika and cayenne pepper.

Cook for a few minutes before adding the tin of tomatoes and water and tomato purée.

Bubble the sauce for 10 more minutes before adding the cauliflower, carrots, potatoes and red pepper slices. Season well.

Cover the casserole and put in the preheated oven for 30–40 minutes until the vegetables are soft.

Just before eating, stir in the yoghurt. As I mentioned above you could decorate with some chopped avocado and chopped cherry tomatoes. Serve with rice.

Lentil & Tomato Stew with Thyme & Kale or Cabbage

This is a delicious stew or hearty soup recipe which can be a vegetarian main or side dish. Or you can add some smoked pancetta cubes in the early stages if you are not worried about it being a vegetarian dish.

Serves 6

2 tablespoons light olive oil
2 medium onions, sliced
250g cubed smoked pancetta (optional)
2 garlic cloves, finely chopped
1 celery stick, finely chopped
1 carrot, finely chopped
250g Puy lentils
250ml chicken stock
1 x 400g tin chopped tomatoes or passata
fresh thyme
salt and freshly ground black pepper
250g chopped kale or cabbage
2 tablespoons chopped flat-leaf parsley

Warm the oil in a large heavy-based pan and gently fry the onions for 10 minutes until soft.

Add the carrot and celery and fry for a further 5 minutes.

Add the washed and rinsed lentils and stir them around until they are nicely covered in oil. Add the garlic.

Stir in the chicken stock, chopped tomatoes and if there is not enough liquid add a little more water to cover.

Add the leaves from a few stems of fresh thyme.

Boil very gently for about 30 minutes – always checking there is enough water.

Add the kale or cabbage and bubble for another few minutes – then stir in the chopped parsley, season to taste and serve.

Spaghetti Aglio e Olio

There is a wonderful restaurant in the Fulham Road, London called 'Aglio e Olio' and I just love it – it is always full and serves the most lovely Italian food. I always choose this Spaghetti Aglio e Olio there and I have tried to copy their dish – it is never quite as nice but this is a good version of it. Have it with a rocket salad with some apple cider vinegar, olive oil and salt – what a simple supper.

Serves 4

450g spaghetti
4 tablespoons extra-virgin olive oil
3 garlic cloves, peeled and very finely sliced
½ red chilli, deseeded and finely chopped (or more to taste)
1 handful chopped flat-leaf parsley
salt and freshly ground black pepper

Cook the pasta following instructions on the packet – various brands differ. I like to use De Cecco.

Put the olive oil in a heavy-based pan with the garlic and chilli – cook until the garlic slightly changes colour but whatever you do don't burn it. Then add the cooked pasta and stir in the flat-leaf parsley and season well.

Vicky's Tomato Tart

Another wonderful recipe from Vicky Hodgkinson, a super lunch dish with a simple mixed leaf salad with some olive oil and cider vinegar.

Serves 6

125g plain flour
125g rolled oats
pinch of salt
125g butter or lard or both mixed
1 egg, beaten

Filling

2 onions, finely sliced
1 large garlic clove, finely chopped
60g butter
1 x 400g tin of tomatoes (I like cherry tomatoes)
2 medium eggs
4 tablespoons double cream
1 tablespoon freshly grated Parmesan
¼ teaspoon cayenne pepper
60g grated cheddar
20g fresh breadcrumbs

Make the pastry by putting the flour, oats, salt, cubed butter or lard into a food processor and pulse until the mixture looks like breadcrumbs.

Add the beaten egg and pulse again until the mixture comes together.

Take the pastry out of the food processor and put in the fridge to cool and harden a bit whilst you do the following.

Preheat the oven to 180°C.

Line a 24cm loose-bottomed tart tin with Bakewell paper.

Melt the butter in a heavy frying pan and gently fry the onions until soft but not brown and then add the garlic and stir around. Add the tin of tomatoes and bubble very slowly to thicken the sauce. Mix the cream with the eggs and season with salt and pepper – add the cayenne pepper to this mixture.

Take the pastry out of the fridge and roll out to put in your prepared tin – prick the base.

Take the tomato sauce off the heat and cool a little before adding the cream and egg mixture. Stir in the Parmesan.

Grate the cheddar over the top, sprinkle with the breadcrumbs and bake in the oven for 30 minutes until the mixture is set.

Spinach & Lentil Dahl

Another vegetarian dish which could be the side dish to a meat or fish curry. I have it for supper with either rice or a flatbread, which sometimes I make or sometimes I buy from a supermarket. I have done this for a client and added cubes of sweet potato, which is good as well.

Serves 4

50g butter
1 onion, finely sliced
2 garlic cloves, finely chopped
4cm fresh ginger, peeled and grated on a coarse grater
2 red chillies, deseeded and finely chopped
1 teaspoon cumin powder
½ teaspoon turmeric
½ teaspoon salt
250g red lentils
1 x 400g tin chopped tomatoes
900ml water
400g fresh spinach, washed

Fry the onion slowly in the butter for about 10 minutes until nice and soft.

Add the garlic, ginger and chillies – stir for another few minutes and then add the cumin, turmeric and salt and stir for another few minutes.

Add the lentils, tomatoes, water and bring slowly to the boil.

Slowly simmer with the lid on for about 20–30 minutes. You will need to check and stir from time to time.

Just before eating, stir in the spinach for a minute until wilted and then serve at once.

Tip If you wanted to add sweet potatoes I would add another 200ml of water at the start and put 2 peeled and chopped sweet potatoes in with the tomatoes and water.

Cauliflower & Potatoes with Indian Spices

This is a lovely vegetarian supper and again you could have it with flatbreads or rice – or you could have it as an accompaniment to any meat curry.

Heat the oil in a heavy-based pan and gently fry the onions until soft for about 10 minutes.

Add the cumin seeds and garlic and fry a little more.

Add the cauliflower and potatoes and fry for another 5 minutes.

Add the ground coriander, turmeric and chilli and stir well.

Add the water and yoghurt and bring gently to the boil and then simmer for 15 minutes until the vegetables are cooked.

Add the chopped coriander leaves, garam masala and cook for another 5 minutes.

Serves 4

3 tablespoons sunflower oil
2 medium onions, finely chopped
2 garlic cloves, crushed
1 teaspoon cumin seeds
1 cauliflower, cut into florets
500g potatoes, peeled and cubed
½ teaspoon ground coriander
1 teaspoon turmeric
1 red chilli, deseeded and finely chopped
150ml water
150g thick natural yoghurt
1 tablespoon roughly chopped coriander leaves
2 teaspoons garam masala
salt

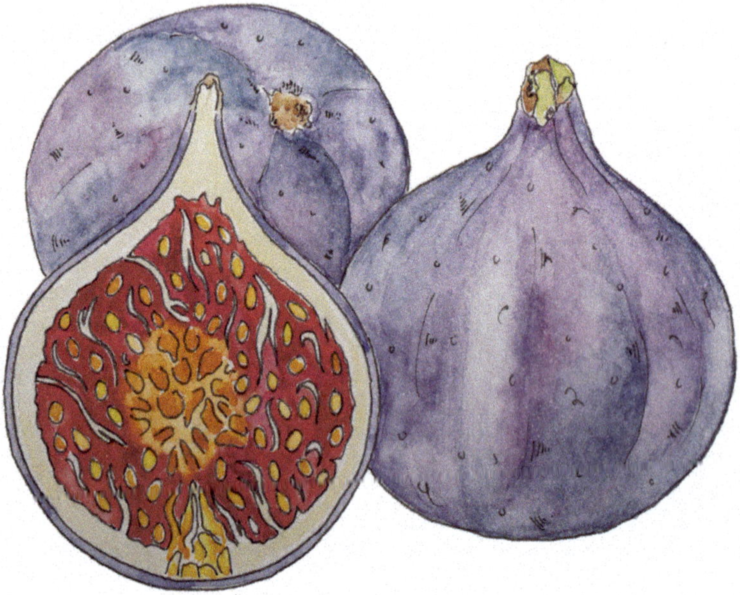

Puddings

A Delicious Crumble

To go with any fruit. I think this is a particularly delicious crumble, which you actually cook before you spread over the fruit base. It is good served with a dollop of vanilla ice cream.

Serves 6

80g plain flour
50g butter, chilled and cut into 2cm cubes
50g light soft brown sugar
pinch of salt
100g walnuts, roughly broken
2 large cooking apples
6 large plums
2 tablespoons light soft brown sugar
pinch of cinnamon
zest of 1 lemon
200g flour
125g butter
100g light soft brown sugar
75g porridge oats

Preheat the oven to 180°C.

Place the flour in a large mixing bowl with the butter, sugar and salt.

Use your fingers to rub the mixture into a breadcrumb texture and then stir in the walnuts.

Spread out on a baking tray lined with baking parchment and place in the oven for 15–20 minutes, until dry and cooked through.

Remove and leave to cool.

Mix the sugar, flour and butter in a large bowl and make a crumbly mix, add oats and leave in the fridge.

Peel and chop the fruit, I leave the skins on the plums – it gives that rich pink colour in the juice.

Put in a pan with a bit of sugar, cinnamon and lemon zest.

Cook on low heat till the fruit is soft.

Place in an oven dish and cover with the topping.

Cook for about 25 minutes or when you feel the top is brown enough for you.

Alaska Crumble Pie

This is the most lovely, simple pudding and you could use raspberries or even blueberries if you can't get redcurrants. If you are having friends for dinner, you could have the base made with the berries in and the egg whites whipped with the sugar. After the main course just scoop the ice cream onto the fruit and biscuit base and then spread the meringue mix evenly over the top and pop in the preheated oven for 5–8 minutes until it is brown on the outside. It is utterly delicious.

Serves 4–6

Crumb case
175g digestive biscuits
75g butter

Filling
3 egg whites
175g caster sugar
125g raspberries, hulled
125g redcurrants, stemmed, or 250g raspberries if you cannot get redcurrants
500ml tub of vanilla ice cream

Crumb the biscuits in a food processor. Alternatively place them between 2 sheets of greaseproof paper and crush with a rolling pin.

Melt the butter in a pan, add the crumbs and stir well.

Evenly press the mixture over the base and sides of a 24cm flan tin and chill until ready to serve.

Whisk the egg whites with an electric mixer in a grease-free bowl until stiff and dry.

Whisk in 1 tablespoon the sugar, then fold in the remainder.

Preheat the oven to 200°C.

When ready to serve, fill the crumb case with the fruit and add scoops of the ice cream.

Spread the meringue over the top, covering the filling completely.

Bake in oven for 6 minutes, until the meringue is golden. Serve immediately.

Almond Tart

This tart is another recipe dedicated to JoJo Palmer, who for years now has always asked me to make a few when her entire family gets together for any occasion. Below is the recipe – you can keep it plain almond or add thinly sliced apples (with their skin on or off) or thinly sliced pears or even fresh apricots – all totally delicious. The sweet pastry you can use for any tart: lemon, chocolate or anything you choose.

Serves 10

350g plain flour
pinch of salt
225g cold butter
100g icing sugar
3 egg yolks

Filling
350g butter, cubed
350g caster sugar
350g ground almonds
4 eggs

Preheat the oven to 180°C.

For the sweet pastry, put the flour, salt and the butter in a food processor and pulse until the mixture resembles coarse breadcrumbs.

Add the sugar then the egg yolks and pulse a bit more.

Take the mixture out of the processor and then press into a tart tin until it is equal all around the tin – about ½cm thick all round.

Bake the pastry in the oven for 20 minutes until crisp.

Reduce the temperature to 150°C.

For the filling, cream the butter and sugar until the mixture is pale and light, then add the eggs one by one.

Slowly stir in the ground almonds and then pour the mixture in the pastry case.

Bake for 40 minutes until firm to the touch – it might need longer depending on your oven.

Apple Amber

I hope you are still enjoying these 'old faithfuls' – here is another from the past. Sometimes these delicious old-fashioned recipes simply can't be beaten.

Serves 6

1kg cooking apples
3 tablespoons water
grated zest of 2 lemons
1 teaspoon cinnamon
75g butter
100g light soft brown sugar
2 medium egg yolks
3 medium egg whites
100g caster sugar
1 tablespoon demerara sugar to dredge the meringue

Preheat the oven to 150°C.

Peel core and slice apples – and put in a pan with water and lemon zest and simmer until soft – drain any excess water.

Liquidise apples until smooth.

Add cinnamon, butter, light soft brown sugar and egg yolks – stir well.

Put the apple mixture into a shallow ovenproof dish and bake gently in oven for about 30 minutes until apple mixture is set.

Turn oven down to 120°C.

Whisk egg whites stiffly and fold in caster sugar – pile it on top of apple mixture and return dish to the oven for about 40 minutes.

Puddings

Baked Peaches (or Nectarines) with Blackcurrants, Mascarpone & Crushed Digestives

This is a lovely simple way of serving peaches or nectarines when they are around in the summer months.

Serves 4

- 4 peaches or nectarines, halved and stoned
- 125g blackcurrants
- 1 tub mascarpone
- 4 tablespoons golden caster sugar
- 6 digestive biscuits, crushed
- 4 tablespoons runny honey

Preheat the oven to 200°C.

If using fresh blackcurrants, remove them from their stalks. Put the blackcurrants in a saucepan and heat with the sugar and a tablespoon water. As the fruits start to burst, remove the pan from the heat.

Place the peaches or nectarines in a shallow ovenproof dish, cut side up, then put a spoonful of the warm blackcurrants in the hollow of each half.

Mix the mascarpone with the crushed digestive biscuits and spoon on top of the blackcurrants.

Drizzle the honey over and bake on a high shelf in the oven until the juices are bubbling and the mascarpone has melted – about 10 minutes.

Serve hot, spooning over the juices from the dish and any remaining blackcurrants.

Blueberry, Coconut & Lime Ice-Cream

This is a great ice cream and is so easy to make. The great thing is you can make it without an ice cream maker or without having to remember to take it out of the freezer regularly to whisk!

Serves 4–6

juice and zest of 2 limes
140g golden caster sugar
125g blueberries
200ml coconut cream
284ml double cream
extra blueberries to serve

Put the lime juice in a small pan with the sugar and heat gently, stirring to dissolve the sugar.

Add the blueberries and simmer for 2 minutes, just until the skins start to split.

Pour the blueberry mixture into a bowl and stir in the coconut cream. Leave to cool.

Whip the double cream in a large bowl until it just holds its shape, then gradually stir in the blueberry mixture.

Put the bowl in the freezer for about 1 hour, until the mixture is set about 3cm in from the edges.

Remove from the freezer and mix it all together using a whisk. When it's fairly smooth, return to the freezer for a further hour.

Repeat the whisking one more time.

Transfer the ice cream to a rigid container, cover and freeze until firm, or for up to a month.

Tip Before serving, move to the fridge for 30 minutes to soften it. Serve with extra blueberries scattered over.

Brilliant Meringue Recipe

Again, there are so many meringue recipes that it is difficult to know which to follow. This one is really good – nothing more delicious than a simple fluffy meringue, either just sandwiched together with thick cream or with lemon curd as well. Sometimes I add a tablespoon of chopped walnuts or pistachios for extra crunch.

Makes 32 small meringues

4 large egg whites
115g caster sugar
115g icing sugar

Preheat the oven to 100°C.

Line 2 baking sheets with non-stick baking paper – never use foil or greaseproof paper or they will stick.

Whisk the egg whites in a very clean bowl of an electric mixer until very stiff.

Add the caster sugar a tablespoon at a time – beating for a few seconds between each addition.

Sift the icing sugar gently over the mixture and fold in gently with a big metal spoon – do not over-mix.

Scoop a pudding spoon of the mixture at a time onto the baking trays and bake for 1½ to 1¾ hours in the oven until the meringues are crisp underneath and are a pale coffee colour.

Leave to cool on the trays or a cooling rack. The meringues will keep in an airtight tin for up to 2 weeks.

Cheat's Rhubarb Crumble Ice Cream

A lovely simple cheat's ice cream. You can replace the biscuits with crushed Crunchie bars instead if you are feeling really indulgent!

Line a 14 x 21cm loaf pan with cling film.

Cook the rhubarb in a saucepan with a lid on, for about 5 minutes with the brown sugar until the rhubarb is tender. Cool.

Place the ice cream in a large bowl and swirl in the biscuits and rhubarb mixture.

Pour the ice cream mixture into the prepared pan and freeze.

Serves 8

220g rhubarb, chopped
2 tablespoons light soft brown sugar
2 litres of Carte d'Or vanilla ice cream or Marks and Spencer Cornish vanilla ice cream
125g ginger biscuits or digestive biscuits, chopped coarsely

Chocolate Biscuit Pudding Cake

This is another of my father's recipes – it is delicious and simple. One of my favourite cold puddings.

Serves 6

250g digestive biscuits
250g dark chocolate
250g butter
2 eggs, beaten
75g caster sugar
50g glace cherries or soft prunes
50g chopped walnuts
optional small glass brandy or rum

Crush the biscuits.

Melt the chocolate with the butter.

Beat the eggs and sugar and then add the melted chocolate mixture.

Stir in the glace cherries, biscuits, walnuts and brandy/rum if using, and then put into a lined loaf tin and leave in fridge until set.

Chocolate Roulade

This is an old-fashioned recipe, but it never fails to please and is proving very popular at weddings once again.

Preheat the oven to 180°C.

Line a 22cm by 32cm baking tray with non-stick paper

Beat yolks until thick and add the sugar and beat thoroughly.

Beat the egg whites until very stiff.

Add the cocoa powder to the sugar and yolk mixture.

Fold in the stiffly beaten egg whites.

Spread the mixture evenly into the baking tray.

Bake in preheated oven for 12 minutes.

Serves 6–8

5 eggs, separated
90g icing sugar
3 tablespoons cocoa
plain flour
250ml whipped cream

Chocolate sauce
Serves 6–8

75g light soft brown sugar
1 pudding spoon cocoa powder
25g butter
1 pudding spoon water

Turn out onto baking paper sprinkled with icing sugar – then cover with a damp tea towel and when cool spread with whipped cream and roll. You can either serve plain or with chocolate sauce as below.

Chocolate Sauce mix the ingredients in a double boiler and keep warm until needed.

Mimi's Chocolate Truffles

This is another recipe I learnt at the cookery school I went to in the 1970s in Victoria, run by a marvellous French lady called Elizabeth Russell. She was fiercely passionate about food and what she taught us was invaluable. Whenever I make these, I think of my niece Mimi, who loved making them.

Makes 40

250g good dark chocolate
225g caster sugar
250g butter
4 medium egg yolks
3 tablespoons of cocoa powder

Beat the egg yolks with the sugar until light in colour.

Melt the chocolate and butter in a bowl on top of a pan of simmering water until melted and mixed together.

Stir in the eggs and sugar mixture with the chocolate and butter.

Chill the chocolate mixture easier if you spread it over a tray and leave in the fridge for when you need to scoop it into truffle shapes.

Sieve cocoa powder on to another tray and once the mixture has hardened in the fridge roll out truffle-size balls and rub into the cocoa.

This also works well as a really rich chocolate sauce before it has set.

Rory's Crème Brûlée

This is the best easy crème brûlée recipe – it is in here for my wonderful nephew Rory who I always think about when anyone serves crème brûlée. Once you have poured over the caramel, let it go hard and then eat it as soon as you can – the caramel sometimes goes soft if left in the fridge too long.

Serves 6

Preheat the oven to 150°C.

Beat together the egg yolks and sugar.

Pour cream onto the egg mixture and stir in a few drops of vanilla essence.

Strain the custard into ramekins (probably 4 or 6).

Stand dish in baking tray containing 2.5cm of hot water and bake for 30 minutes or until firm to the touch.

Leave in refrigerator or somewhere cold overnight.

For the caramel topping, preheat the grill to its highest setting and spoon granulated sugar over the top of each ramekin – put the ramekins under the grill until the sugar caramelises and leave to cool before eating.

4 egg yolks
60g caster sugar
½ pint double cream
½ pint single cream
a few drops vanilla essence

Caramel topping
90g granulated sugar

Simple Orange & Yoghurt Cheesecake with Pistachios

This is another favourite of our team and we have served it at so many weddings. To make it look pretty and taste even more delicious you can serve it with some finely sliced oranges in their juices sprinkled with coarsely chopped pistachios.

Serves 8

200g digestive biscuits
100g butter, melted
500g full cream yoghurt
250g mascarpone
250ml double cream
120ml good runny honey
zest and juice of 1 large orange
1 sachet powdered gelatine
1 tablespoon chopped pistachios
2 large oranges to decorate

Take a 26cm cake tin with a removable base, grease with a bit of soft butter and then line with non-stick paper.

Put the biscuits and butter into the drum of a blender and pulse until no lumps can be seen. Push the mixture into the cake tin.

Put the tin in the fridge for about an hour until it is completely set.

To make the topping, whisk the double cream until thick and then gently stir in the yoghurt and mascarpone until well mixed.

Add the honey and orange zest.

Stir the gelatine into the juice of the orange in a small heavy-based pan. Put this over a very low heat and watch until the gelatine is dissolved.

Pour the mixture into the cream mixture and then pour the whole lot over the biscuit base.

Put in a fridge for at least 5 hours to set.

Eton Mess

Again, I am sure you all have this recipe but as so many Brides and Grooms ask for this as their pudding I thought I should include it. I may say that one Bride was horrified that I had "such an old-fashioned idea on the pudding menu as Eton Mess" – but I think some people are missing the point about good food. How lovely in summer to be served a delicious, zingy and brightly coloured Eton Mess as a pudding. Please don't attempt to do this with out-of-season, imported, tasteless strawberries. Do use shop-bought meringue nests as they hold their crunch longer than homemade ones.

Serves 4

225g frozen raspberries, defrosted
55g icing sugar
450g English strawberries
150ml double cream
150ml Greek full-fat yoghurt
4 shop-bought meringue nests, crumbled

Put the defrosted raspberries in a food processor and purée with the icing sugar until smooth.

Sieve to remove the seeds.

Whip together the double cream and yoghurt.

Cut the strawberries into equal sized bits and stir into cream and yoghurt mixture, along with the crumbled meringue nests.

Stir in the raspberry purée and serve in individual glass dishes – perhaps with some homemade shortbread.

Gooseberry (or any soft fruit) Fool

I thought I had finished my cookery book recipes and then I remembered so many from years ago, that I just had to put in this foolproof one. It is another of my favourites.

Serves 6

500g gooseberries, topped and tailed
250g caster sugar
250ml double cream, whipped
200ml water
1 egg white, whisked until firm

Put the gooseberries in the water and bubble for 8 minutes until soft.

Drain from the water and liquidise with the sugar.

Cool the mixture in the fridge.

When cool, fold in the whipped cream and the whisked egg white. Keep cool in the fridge until you want to eat it.

You could also use strawberries or raspberries, but you would not need to cook the fruit first.

Lemon Amaretti Cream Pots

I am all for spooning out this pudding from a vast dish in the centre of the table, but there is an elegance and style about a pudding served in small individual dishes – like those classic French chocolate mousse pots.

Serves 8

275g lemon curd, homemade or luxury shop-bought
110g amaretti or ratafia biscuits
284ml double cream
250g thick natural yoghurt

Pour the double cream into a cold china bowl and whisk it gently until it starts to thicken.

Now fold in the yoghurt and lemon curd with a large metal spoon.

Put the amaretti or ratafia biscuits in a plastic bag and crush them carefully with a heavy object. You are after large crumbs and small lumps – the size of gravel – rather than fine breadcrumbs. Fold these into the cream.

Scrape into 8 small classic French chocolate mousse pots or espresso cups (small ramekins will do) and cover tightly with cling film.

Refrigerate for at least two hours. This will allow time for the biscuits to soften a little and the flavours to infuse.

Lemon Chiffon

An original recipe we used to serve our chalet guests in Méribel in 1975 – it was always popular but seems to have been forgotten in favour of the more modern and delicious lemon posset! It does need to be kept cold in a fridge until you want to eat it.

Serves 6

2 teaspoons of powder gelatine
3 tablespoons of cold water
4 eggs, separated
2 large lemons
5 tablespoons sugar
pinch of salt

Put the cold water into a cup and sprinkle over the gelatine.

Using a small bowl, grate the lemon zest using a very fine grater and squeeze in the juice.

Separate the eggs.

Whisk the sugar with the egg yolks until pale and put in a bowl on top of a simmering saucepan or in the top of a double boiler.

Add the juice of the lemons, the zest and the gelatine and whisk until the mixture froths.

Let it cool a bit whilst you whisk the egg whites until stiff and then fold into the lemon mixture gently with a spoon.

Place in a serving dish and put into fridge until set.

Lemon Posset with Lemon Shortbread

I am sure everyone has a recipe for lemon posset, but I love it so much as a simple little pudding, that I could not leave this one out.

Serves 6

For the posset
600ml double cream
150g caster sugar
zest and juice of 4 lemons

Shortbread
90g icing sugar
185g plain flour
60g cornflour
30g ground almonds
250g butter, cut into cubes, plus extra for greasing
a few drops of almond essence
75g lemon curd, homemade or luxury shop-bought
icing sugar for dusting

Place the double cream and the sugar into a large pan over a low heat and bring to the boil slowly. Boil for three minutes, then remove from the heat and allow to cool.

Add the lemon zest and juice and whisk well.

Pour the lemon cream mixture into six large serving glasses and refrigerate for three hours.

Shortbread: Preheat the oven to 180°C.

Sift the icing sugar, flour and cornflour together into a bowl and add the ground almonds.

Transfer the flour mixture to a food processor.

Add the butter and pulse until there are no visible lumps of butter.

Add the almond essence. Pulse again then turn the mixture out onto a lightly floured surface and knead a few times, to form a smooth dough.

Grease a muffin tray with butter.

Divide the dough up and roll into small balls. Place the balls into the muffin cups, flattening the tops slightly with your fingers. The dough should come about one third of the way up the side of each muffin cup to give a nice proportion to the finished biscuit.

Transfer to the oven and bake for 8–12 minutes, until they are a light golden colour.

Remove from the oven, allow to cool slightly, then, using your thumb, make a small indentation into the top of each biscuit.

Let the shortbreads cool for a few minutes, then turn the mould over and tap the shortbreads out. (Be gentle, as the biscuits are fragile while they are still warm.)

When all the shortbreads are baked and cooled, dust the tops with icing sugar.

Little Chocolate Pots

This is the richest little pot of chocolate you will ever eat. You need to allow a crust to form towards the end of cooking which sometimes looks as if you have overcooked it – but it adds to the wonderful texture.

Serves 4

175ml double cream
a drop of good vanilla essence
125g dark chocolate
75ml whole milk
2 small egg yolks
1 heaped tablespoon icing sugar

Preheat the oven to 140°C.

Warm the double cream with the vanilla essence and leave to infuse for half an hour.

Melt the chocolate in the milk in another pan.

Mix the egg yolks with the icing sugar in a bowl and then blend with the chocolate milk mixture and the double cream.

Pour the mixture into 4 ramekins.

Put the ramekins into a deep baking dish.

Pour boiling water into the baking dish so it comes halfway up the sides of the ramekins.

Bake in the oven for 45 minutes.

Cool in the fridge for at least 5 hours before serving.

Little Raspberry Jellies

These are very easy to make and look rather special and are particularly good for people who don't want a creamy heavier pudding. The raspberries can be replaced with mixed summer fruit and the rosé with a sparkling white wine.

Makes 6

700g raspberries
300ml sparkling rosé wine or sparkling white wine
20g leaf gelatine
150g granulated sugar

Cover the raspberries with the wine and steep for 15 minutes.

Soak the gelatine in cold water for 5 minutes.

Dissolve the sugar in a pan with 300ml water over a low heat.

Bring to the boil and boil for 2 minutes.

Remove the gelatine, squeezing out excess water, and stir into the hot sugar syrup to dissolve.

Carefully drain the raspberries, reserving the wine, and divide the fruit between 6 x 150ml moulds.

Combine the wine and syrup, then pour into the moulds.

Chill overnight.

Tip To turn out, loosen with a palette knife and briefly dip the base of the mould into hot water. Put a plate on top and turn over. A sharp shake should release any reluctant jellies.

Mummy's Spiced Pears

(Bridget Jackson's Mummy!)
My friend Bridget and I have always had the same taste in good simple food and this is a recipe she gave me, which is delicious served with a Victoria sandwich cake (made with almonds instead of flour) or with vanilla ice cream.

Serves 6

900g firm pears
150ml water
110g granulated sugar
150ml red wine
1 cinnamon stick
zest of 1 lemon

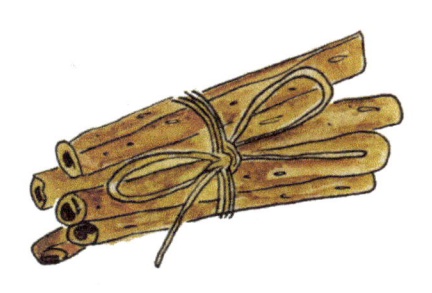

Slice pears very finely – I use firm Williams. Do not use soft fruit, it just collapses.

Make syrup with water, sugar and red wine. Add cinnamon stick and lemon zest then add the pears.

Poach the pears until they are transparent, then remove from syrup.

Boil the juice hard until almost sticky. Pour over the pears.

Remove cinnamon stick but leave lemon rind.

Serve chilled.

Nectarine Blueberry Crisp

Probably 30 years ago I went to North Dakota on a work trip with an old friend, 'Fungus', who sadly died in his early 50s. He was not remotely interested in food but we went with Amanda and Nick Rowe who, like me, loved to discuss what we were eating. The food was interesting there and I had this delicious pudding and managed to get the recipe from the ranch – I could not recommend it more.

Serves 6

Topping
150g plain flour
65g light brown soft sugar
65g granulated sugar
pinch of salt
¼ teaspoon ground cinnamon
½ teaspoon ground ginger
150g cold butter, cubed

Filling
750g firm, ripe nectarines
500g blueberries
¼ cup caster sugar
2 tablespoons plain flour

Preheat the oven to 180°C.

For the topping – mix all the dry ingredients and spices together in a mixing bowl and then cut the butter into the mixture until it looks like fine breadcrumbs.

For the filling – de-stone the nectarines and cut into thick slices.

Toss the nectarines in a bowl with the blueberries, caster sugar and flour.

Put the fruit into a medium-sized oven-proof dish and sprinkle the topping over the fruit.

Bake in the oven for 25–30 minutes or until the top is brown and bubbling around the edge.

Remove from the oven and cool for at least 15 minutes before serving.

Orange & Almond Cake

There are many versions of this orange and almond cake but this one works brilliantly and I love it, so I thought it deserved a place in my book.

Preheat the oven to 200°C.

Line a 26cm round removable bottomed cake tin with Bakewell paper.

To cook the oranges, place them in a pan and cover generously with water. Put a lid on, bring to the boil and simmer steadily until completely soft – about 1 hour.

2 whole oranges, skin on
250g caster sugar
250g softened butter
6 eggs, separated
300g ground almonds
1 tablespoon baking powder
icing sugar to dust

Cool the oranges and then cut in half and remove any pips. Put the oranges in a food processor with the sugar, butter, egg yolks, almonds and baking powder and pulse until well combined.

Whisk the egg whites until soft peaks form and then fold in the orange mixture until the two mixtures are evenly combined.

Put the mixture into the prepared tin and bake for 10 minutes, reducing the temperature to 160°C for another 50 minutes.

Cool on wire rack in its tin for 10 minutes before unmoulding.

Dust lavishly with icing sugar and serve cut into slices with crème fraîche.

Tip You can make this cake a couple of days in advance and you can make it more of a 'dinner party' dish by serving each slice in a pool of citrus syrup – use the zest and juice of 3 oranges and 1 lemon, 125g sugar and 125ml water. Simmer all together for about 20 minutes.

Perfect Chocolate Mousse Recipe

There are so many Chocolate Mousse recipes which have cream in, which I think completely spoils it. This one, in my view, is just perfect.

Serves 6

250g Bournville chocolate, chopped into pieces
1 small cup of water or black coffee
50g butter
6 eggs, separated

Melt chocolate in double pan over simmering water and add butter and water/coffee.

Draw off the heat and beat in the yolks of the eggs one by one.

Whisk the egg whites until stiff with an electric whisk and stir briskly into the chocolate.

Place mixture into individual ramekins and leave in fridge overnight.

Pistachio Ice Cream

This is a wonderful ice cream – very easy to make and does not need an ice cream maker or whisking whilst it is setting in the freezer. I love anything with pistachios and the saltiness with the sugar is an excellent combination. Serve with the berry compote.

Serves 8

Ice cream
275g salted pistachios with shells removed
150g caster sugar
4 large egg whites
400ml double cream

Berry compote
300g frozen blueberries
4 tablespoons water
25g caster sugar

Pulse 100g pistachio kernels with 25g sugar in a food processor until finely ground. Add the remaining pistachios and pulse once or twice to break up roughly.

Using an electric whisk, whisk the egg whites until stiff – fold in the remaining sugar until the mixture is stiff and glossy.

Whip the double cream until it is stiff – not too stiff, just until it holds its shape.

Using a metal spoon fold in the egg whites and then the pistachios.

Pour the mixture into a plastic container and freeze for 5 hours at least.

To make the compote – gently warm the blueberries in a pan with the water and caster sugar and bubble for 5 minutes until the berries release their juices.

Take the ice cream out of the freezer 10 minutes before you are ready to eat it.

Poached Pears with Fudge Sauce

This is a wonderfully old-fashioned, but delicious, recipe and children love it!

Serves 4

- 225g granulated sugar
- 2 cinnamon sticks
- 4 medium-sized firm pears, peeled but stalks intact
- 50g butter
- 75g light soft brown sugar
- 30ml golden syrup
- 50ml double cream

Place the granulated sugar and the cinnamon sticks in a pan, add 500ml water and heat gently, stirring occasionally, until the sugar dissolves.

Bring to the boil and bubble for 2 minutes.

Meanwhile, carefully remove the core from the pears using the tip of a vegetal peeler or the sharp edge of a teaspoon.

Place the pears immediately in the sugar syrup and cover the pan with a circle of greaseproof paper, followed by a lid.

Bring the pears to the boil, reduce the heat and cook gently for 20–25 minutes or until tender. Set aside.

Place the butter, brown sugar, syrup and cream in a pan. Heat gently until melted, then bring to the boil and bubble for 1 minute.

Lift the pears out of the syrup and spoon the warm fudge sauce over. Serve immediately.

Queen of Puddings

A delicious and very economical pudding to make – although very old-fashioned it is always popular. You can use marmalade or any jam you like!

Serves about 4–6

600ml full-fat milk
600g white breadcrumbs
50g butter
grated zest of 2 lemons
50g granulated sugar
3 eggs, separated
3 tablespoons orange marmalade or jam
75g caster sugar
15g butter

Preheat the oven to 150°C.

Heat the milk and when it is hot, add the breadcrumbs, butter, lemon zest and granulated sugar and leave it to soak for 30 minutes.

Separate the eggs and beat the egg yolks into the bread mixture.

Butter an ovenproof shallow dish and pour the mixture into it.

Bake it in oven for 30 minutes.

Remove from the oven and spread the jam or marmalade over it.

Whisk the egg whites until stiff and then stir in the sugar gently and spread over the pudding.

Bake in very cool oven at 120°C for 1 hour.

Salted Caramel Chocolate Tart

This is so good – you can either make your own sweet pastry or buy some ready-made sweet pastry from a supermarket and roll it out to line a 30cm loose-bottomed flan tin. Bake the pastry blind and cool before filling it with the caramel and chocolate as below.

Serves 8

For the caramel
220g light soft brown sugar
250ml double cream
125g chopped butter
½ teaspoon Maldon salt

For the chocolate layer
100g caster sugar
2 eggs
2 egg yolks
250g dark chocolate
150g butter, cubed

Put all the caramel ingredients into a small heavy pan and bring slowly to the boil.

Take off heat and leave to cool.

For the chocolate layer Preheat the oven to 180°C.

Whisk sugar, eggs and yolks until thick and creamy.

Gently melt the chocolate and butter together, leave to cool.

Add it to the egg and sugar mixture, whisking until glossy.

Spread the caramel over the pastry base then spoon over the chocolate mixture and bake for 20 minutes or until it is almost set but still a bit wobbly.

Scrummy Pear & Ginger Tart

I have never pretended to be a modern cook and do not accept that some of these wonderful old-fashioned recipes are "old hat", especially when they are as good as something like this. Small children will love it!

Serves 6

250g ginger biscuits
125g butter, melted
175g caster sugar
500ml water
3 large ripe pears
450ml double cream, whipped
1 tablespoon icing sugar

Caramel sauce
220g light soft brown sugar
250g double cream
125g butter

Crush the biscuits in a food processor or similar until well ground and add the melted butter.

Line a loose-bottomed tart – 26cm wide – with non-stick paper and press the biscuit mixture into the tin.

Put in the fridge to harden for 30 minutes.

Whip the double cream with the icing sugar and set aside.

Place caster sugar and water into a saucepan and stir over low heat to dissolve the sugar.

Peel the pears with a potato peeler and leave them whole – put them into the sugar syrup mixture and simmer for 10 minutes until the fruit is cooked.

Cool the fruit in the syrup.

Once cool take the pears out and slice thinly – if too wet, dry them on some kitchen paper.

Lay the pieces over the biscuit base and then cover with the whipped cream and icing sugar.

Make the caramel sauce by stirring the light soft brown sugar, double cream and butter together until the sugar dissolves. Dribble the sauce over the cream.

Simple Cheesecake Recipe From Forty Years Ago

This is delicious and so easy – another from my chalet girl days.

Serves 6–8

1 large tin evaporated milk
250g full-fat cream cheese
50g caster sugar
1 packet of lemon jelly
150ml boiling water
zest and juice of 1 lemon
200g digestive biscuits
50g butter, melted

Chill the tin of evaporated milk and beat until double in quantity.

Cream the cheese with the sugar until soft.

Dissolve the lemon jelly in 150ml boiling water and add the lemon juice and zest. Cool this mixture.

Add the jelly and cream cheese to the evaporated milk and mix well.

Crush the biscuits finely and melt the butter – mix together and line a 26cm cake tin with the biscuit crumbs.

Chill for 10 minutes in the fridge.

Pour over the cheese mixture and chill again.

Spiced Tropical Brûlée

This is a lovely light pudding – particularly good on a nice summer day. Jenny Brown, a very old friend of mine, gave it to me – she really is a fabulous cook and is Australian so always calls me with some new recipe she has found in an Australian magazine – they are all excellent.

Serves 6–8

100g granulated sugar
4 star anise
1 lemon
1 mango, skinned and chopped
1 medium or small pineapple, skinned and chopped
12 lychees (or physalis)
2 bananas, sliced
2 passion fruit, squeezed

Topping

425ml double cream, or a mix of whipped double cream and full-fat Greek yoghurt
85g granulated sugar

Place sugar in a small saucepan with 100ml water and the star anise.

Finely pare 3 strips of lemon rind and add to the syrup.

Set over a low heat, stirring occasionally, until the sugar has dissolved and simmer gently for 10 minutes.

Prepare fruit, seed physalis and cut in half, add all the fruit to the syrup mixture.

Whip the double cream and stir in the yoghurt if using.

Spoon the whipped cream mixture over the fruit in the serving dish.

Meanwhile, place sugar in a saucepan with 5 tablespoons boiling water. Set over low heat and stir occasionally until sugar has dissolved, then turn the heat up high and boil vigorously until it begins to caramelise and turn golden brown. Take it off the heat – it will continue to cook.

As soon as it is a rich brown, slowly drizzle the boiling hot caramel over the cream topping of the pudding. Chill until needed.

Sticky Toffee Pudding

We have done this pudding so many times at a wedding and people just love it – the sticky toffee sauce is particularly good – it is so easy to make. I have people book me for another wedding on the basis of this pudding. You can freeze both the pudding and the sauce, to defrost and just reheat!

Serves 12

320g dried pitted dates
375ml hot water
1 teaspoon bicarbonate of soda
95g butter, chopped
250g light soft brown sugar
3 medium eggs
225g self raising flour
60g chopped walnuts

Sticky toffee sauce
220g light soft brown sugar
250ml double cream
125g chopped butter

Preheat oven to 170°C.

Line a tin 38 x 20cm with baking paper.

Put the dates and water into a saucepan. Bring to the boil.

Remove from the heat and stir in the bicarbonate of soda.

Stand for 5 minutes.

Blend the mixture until smooth.

Beat the butter and sugar in a large bowl with an electric mixer until light and fluffy.

Add the eggs one at a time. Continue beating.

Stir in the date mixture and flour.

Spread the mixture into the prepared tin and sprinkle with the nuts.

Bake for 35 minutes, then check with a skewer to see if it is cooked through. Leave to cool in the tin.

To reheat, cover the pudding with greaseproof paper and foil and reheat in hot oven at 170°C for 20 minutes.

Make the toffee sauce: put the sugar, cream and butter into a saucepan and stir until melted and sugar dissolved, without boiling.

Serve the pudding in squares with the sauce spooned over the top.

Sweet Shortcrust Pastry

This is a really easy pastry for any sweet tart recipe.

Preheat the oven to 180°C.

Place the flour, salt and butter in a food processor until the mixture resembles coarse breadcrumbs.

350g plain flour
pinch of salt
225g cold butter, cut into cubes
100g icing sugar, sifted
3 egg yolks

Add the icing sugar and then the egg yolks and pulse. The mixture will immediately combine and leave the sides of the bowl.

Wrap the mixture in cling film and leave to cool in fridge for 30 minutes.

Coarsely grate the pastry into a 30cm loose-bottomed flan tin and then press it evenly on to the sides and base.

Bake blind for 20 minutes.

Treacle Tart

Treacle tart always reminds me of when I first moved to London from Jersey and was flat-sharing with Liz, who still works with me now. We used to have friends for supper and would serve them fried mince, treacle tart and Chianti (holding back the bottle as a make-shift candlestick). Clearly, no one was into healthy eating back then!

Pastry
225g plain flour
110g chilled and diced butter
1 medium egg
1 tablespoon icing sugar, sieved

Filling
450g golden syrup (softened over a pan of simmering water)
85g fresh white breadcrumbs
zest of 1 lemon
2 tablespoons lemon juice

Pre-heat the oven to 180°C.

Rub the butter into the flour until it resembles fine breadcrumbs. Then add in the icing sugar and egg with a knife. Knead to a fine dough.

Roll the pastry out thinly onto a floured worktop and use to line a 24cm loose-bottomed tart tin. Put in the fridge to rest for 30 minutes.

Bake the pastry for 15 minutes until golden brown.

Mix together the golden syrup, breadcrumbs, lemon zest and juice. Spoon the filling onto the tart base.

Return the tart to the oven for 25 minutes until set.

The Best Lemon Meringue Pie

When looking up lemon meringue pie recipes, I always found there was not enough lemon juice in, so I multiplied the lemon juice and now think I have the perfect recipe. If you don't like making pastry do use a ready-made bought one.

Put the flour, icing sugar and salt in the food processor and pulse to mix.

Then add the butter cubes and pulse until the mixture resembles fine breadcrumbs.

Add the yolks and whole eggs.

Take the dough out of the food processor and push it with your fingers into your pastry tin – a 30cm large loose-bottomed one.

Flatten it all around so it forms a nice thin base and covers the sides. Put the tin in the fridge to cool. If there is too much pastry you could line a small tin and keep in freezer for future use, or just wrap the pastry, label and freeze it until you need it.

To precook the pastry, heat your oven to 180°C and bake the pastry blind with some Bakewell paper on top and weighted down with baking beans (if

Serves 8 (if not more)

Pastry
500g plain flour
100g icing sugar, sifted
Pinch of salt
250g fridge-cold butter, cut into small chunks
2 whole eggs
2 egg yolks, beaten

For the filling
zest and juice of 6 lemons
50g cornflour
475ml water
250g golden caster sugar
6 egg yolks (keep the whites for the topping)

Meringue
6 egg whites
350g caster sugar

you have them or just some old forks if not) for about 25 minutes until it is pale brown and crisp.

Remove from the oven and cool.

For the filling Mix the lemon zest, lemon juice and cornflour until it is a smooth cream.

Boil the water in a saucepan and then add the lemon cream – stirring all the time and bring to the boil.

Separately mix the yolks and sugar and then take the pan off the heat and mix in very slowly the yolk and sugar mixture.

Put back on the heat and stir gently until the sauce thickens like custard.

Set aside to cool and then pour into the prepared pastry base.

Meringue topping

Preheat the oven to 170°C.

Whisk the 6 egg whites with an electric whisk in a clean bowl until stiff and then whisk in the sugar, a tablespoon at a time, until the mixture is shiny and stiff.

Spoon it on to the lemon pie and bake in the preheated oven for 20–25 minutes until the meringue is crispy and brown.

Tarte Tatin

I am sure everyone has a recipe for the wonderful French Tarte Tatin, but I have to admit we had a bride who was going to be happy only if we did Tarte Tatin for 150 at her wedding. So, I thought we had better get practising and it was patient Liz, with Nat helping, who devised this perfect recipe – after many disasters! It is worth buying a special Tarte Tatin tin for this recipe – they are usually about 24cm in diameter – or use a heavy frying pan of about that size with an ovenproof handle.

Serves 8

200g shop-bought ready rolled frozen puff pastry
100g butter
250g caster sugar
1.3kg Cox or any good eating apples
1 lemon

Preheat the oven to 180°C.

Peel and cut the apples in half.

Melt the butter over a low heat in the pan you are going to make the Tatin in.

Add the sugar and stir with a wooden spoon for about 5 minutes or until the sugar begins to caramelise.

Add the apples cut side up – sprinkle with lemon juice and cook slowly for 25 minutes – watching to make sure the sugar does not burn. Then put the tin in oven for 5 minutes.

Take tin out of the oven and cover with the ready rolled pastry – tucking down the edges.

Place in the hot oven for 25 minutes until the pastry is golden brown.

Take out of the oven and place on a wire rack to cool for about 25 minutes before turning out. Serve warm with delicious ice cream.

Tiramisu

Bucket (Helen Prescot), an old friend of mine, who is a wonderful pastry chef, gave me this recipe years ago. She always did make the most delicious puddings I think I have ever eaten and birthday cakes – especially chocolate ones. Sadly, she has now retired.

Serves 4

275g mascarpone cheese
40g caster sugar
½ teaspoon vanilla essence
2 eggs, separated
150ml freshly made good coffee
150ml Marsala or sweet sherry
18 sponge fingers
1 tablespoon cocoa powder

Whisk the cheese, sugar, vanilla and yolks together until light and frothy.

Whisk the egg whites until very firm and fold them into the yolk and sugar mixture.

Mix coffee with the Marsala.

Put a few spoonfuls of cheese mixture into your preferred serving dish – preferably glass.

Dip 2–3 sponge fingers in coffee mixture for 10–15 seconds. Place on top of the cheese mixture. Layer up, finishing with the cheese mixture.

Sift with cocoa powder.

Cover and chill overnight.

Walnut Shortbread

These are a fantastic addition to any pudding – especially something like chocolate mousse or lemon posset, or even just with a cup of coffee. You may think 45 minutes is too long to cook shortbread but at the lower temperature of 150°C it works perfectly.

Makes about 20

120g butter at room temperature
60g caster sugar
180g plain flour, sifted
60g rice flour
60g walnut pieces
a little icing sugar for dusting

Preheat the oven to 150°C.

You will need a baking sheet, lightly greased and a 4.5cm cutter.

Firstly, grind the walnuts, which you can do very carefully using the 'pulse' switch on a food processor (if this is overdone the nuts go pasty and oily). Otherwise a hand-held nut grinder will do the job.

To make the shortbread, place the butter and sugar in a large mixing bowl and cream them together until pale and fluffy.

Then mix the sifted flour and rice flour together and gradually work this into the creamed mixture, a tablespoon at a time.

Next add the ground walnuts and use your hands to form the mixture into a smooth dough.

Leave the dough to rest in a plastic bag in the refrigerator for 30 minutes, then roll it out on a lightly floured working surface to roughly 20cm in diameter.

Now using a 4.5cm cutter, cut out about 20 rounds, re-rolling the trimmings.

Place on a lightly greased baking sheet and bake in the oven for 45 minutes.

Cool the shortbreads for 5 minutes before transferring to a wire rack.

When completely cool, dust them with icing sugar and store in an airtight container.

White Chocolate & Blueberry or Raspberry Cheesecake

This is a very popular pudding and actually freezes well. So easy to make and wonderful with extra blueberries or raspberries on top.

Serves 12

For the base
75g digestive biscuits, crushed
75g ginger biscuits, crushed
75g salted butter, melted

For the filling
400g white chocolate broken into pieces
65g butter
½ teaspoon vanilla extract
500g full-fat cream cheese
50g caster sugar
180ml whipping cream
150g blueberries or raspberries

Combine biscuits and butter. Press onto the base of 24cm springform tin and cool in fridge.

Place chocolate, butter and vanilla in heatproof bowl and melt. Cool slightly.

Meanwhile mix the cream cheese, sugar and whipping cream until smooth and thickened then stir the chocolate mixture into cream.

Gently stir in raspberries, being careful not to release their juice.

Spoon the mixture on top of the biscuit base and put in fridge for at least 8 hours.

Pistachio & Orange Tart

This is really wonderful. Nat, one of my chefs, did it for me once and she now can't remember where she found it or who gave it to her – but it is rich and delicious. You don't need too much so I would think this tart would serve 8 people adequately. I buy my pistachios from the wonderful Iranian shop by the Kingston Bypass – there are many others around London and I know several in Shepherd's Bush. You could always make some meringues with the leftover egg whites or freeze them in ice cube trays so you can take them out in future when you need egg whites.

Preheat the oven to 180°C.

You will need a tart tin: 24cm with a removable base.

Make the pastry by putting the flour and sugar in the bowl of your food processor with the butter and pulse for a minute.

Then add the egg yolks and pulse for another minute.

Take the pastry out of the food processor and refrigerate until chilled and hard.

Take it out and roll on a floured board or work surface until it is big enough to fit into your 24cm tart tin.

Put it in the tin and back in the fridge to firm up again.

Serves 6–8

Pastry base
225g plain flour
250g butter, cut into cubes
2 egg yolks
50g icing sugar

Filling
250g ground almonds
250g ground pistachios
250g caster sugar
¼ teaspoon cardamom powder (buy from a Middle Eastern shop or grind the seeds from 15 cardamom pods to a powder in a coffee grinder)
150ml freshly squeezed orange juice
4 egg yolks
grated zest of 2 oranges

Put the pastry base, lined with baking paper and baking beans, into your hot oven for 20 minutes until the pastry is golden brown.

Let the pastry cool whilst you make the filling – put the ground pistachio, almonds, sugar and cardamom powder in the food processor and pulse.

Pour in the orange juice slowly with the machine on and add the orange zest.

Let the mixture cool a bit and then put the machine back on and add the egg yolks and blend until they are well mixed.

Put the mixture into the cooled base and bake in the oven for 15 minutes until a crust is formed.

Almond, Polenta & Lemon Cake

So many of my recipes remind me of people and I love that. This one reminds me of Fiona Potter – not sure why but I know she loves it. The original recipe came from the River Café book but I have adapted it a bit.

Preheat the oven to 150°C.

Beat the butter and sugar together with an electric whisk until light and fluffy.

Stir in the ground almonds and beat in the eggs one at a time.

Fold in the lemon zest, juice, polenta, baking powder and salt.

Spread the cake into a 26cm cake tin with loose bottom and cook for 45 minutes and then check. It might take an hour.

Take out of the oven and cool in the tin.

Serves 10

300g butter
300g caster sugar
300g ground almonds
4 eggs
zest of 3 lemons
juice of 1 lemon
225g polenta
1½ teaspoon baking powder
½ teaspoon sea salt

Apple & Amaretti Tart

If you like amaretti you will like this one – the base just makes a change from the normal pastry. You need to make this in advance so the pastry cools and absorbs the hot apple juices which gives you a delicious shortbread type base. It looks good and tastes lovely. I think good vanilla ice cream with it is perfect.

Serves 6–8

Base
40g amaretti biscuits
110g plain flour
50g butter
50g caster sugar

Topping
700g green eating apples or evenly sized Bramley apples
10g caster sugar
½ teaspoon cinnamon
25g butter, melted

Preheat the oven to 180°C.

Use a 24cm loose-bottomed tart tin – lined with greaseproof paper.

To make the base: put all the ingredients into your food processor and pulse until it looks like pastry or shortbread – push this mixture into lined tart tin.

For the topping – peel, core and slice the apples thinly. Arrange the thin slices on top of the pastry – make sure the apple slices overlap.

Mix the cinnamon and sugar together in a small bowl and brush the tart generously with the melted butter – then sprinkle the cinnamon and sugar over the top and bake in the hot oven for 40 minutes.

Allow the tart to cool in its tin.

Vicky's Rhubarb & Almond Cake with Flaked Almonds

Vicky Hodgkinson and I always chat on the telephone about food and it is a complete treat to go to her lovely home in Battersea and dine. Her food is always perfect and wonderfully cooked and a lot of time goes into the planning – everything is delicious. This is a recipe she sent me and I tried it with my husband and son and we finished it in one night, it was so good!

Serves 8

400g English rhubarb, trimmed and cut into 2cm pieces (or canned if fresh is not available)
200g caster sugar
150g soft butter or margarine
2 medium eggs, beaten
74g self raising flour
½ teaspoon baking powder
100g ground almonds
zest of 1 orange and 2 tablespoons juice
25g flaked almonds

Preheat the oven to 170°C.

Grease and line with baking parchment a 26cm cake tin.

Put the rhubarb into a bowl with 50g of the sugar and leave for 30 minutes whilst you make the cake.

Using an electric whisk, beat the remaining sugar and soft butter until creamy and pale.

Whisk in the eggs and a tablespoon of flour – don't worry if it curdles a little.

Fold in the remaining flour, baking powder and ground almonds.

Add the orange zest and juice.

Stir the rhubarb and the sugary juices into the cake mixture and put into the prepared tin.

Sprinkle on the flaked almonds and bake in the preheated oven for 45 minutes or until firm.

Leave to cool in the tin for 10 minutes. Best served warm with thick cream or even custard.

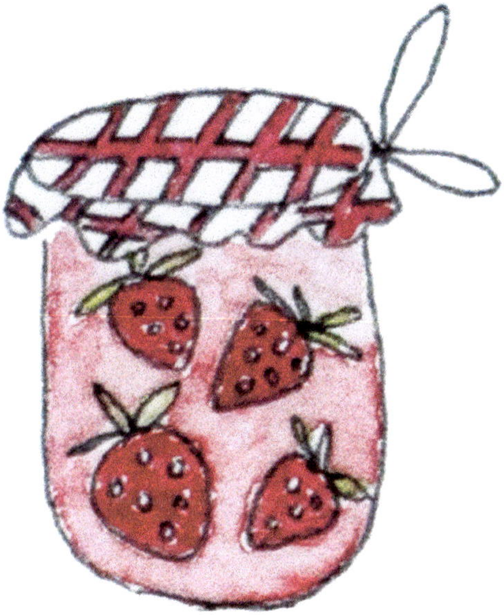

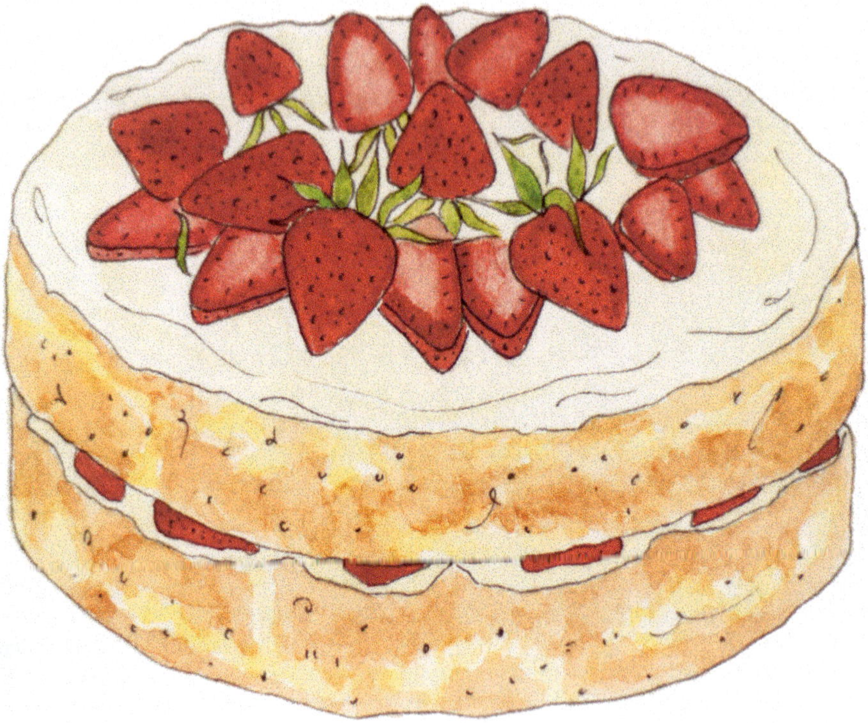

Cakes & Baking

I have put a note in my rules at the start of the book, but I just thought I should add some thoughts here. With baking, so much depends on the oven you are using, as all ovens vary so much. So, when my recommended timings are up, always take the cake/brownies out of the oven and test with a skewer in the middle. If the skewer comes out clean then the cake mixture is ready, if not, just pop the cake back in the oven for another 5 minutes and continue this until the skewer comes out clean.

See also recipes for Orange & Almond Cake, Walnut Shortbreads, Almond Polenta Cake and Rhubarb & Almond Cake in the Pudding section.

Chesty's Hunting Cake (Helen Mullens)

This is a superb recipe from my old friend Chesty and it works beautifully – I always cook it in a brownie tin (32cm by 20cm) lined with Bakewell paper.

320g butter
320g mixture of sultanas, raisins, currants (any dried fruit will do)
320g light soft brown sugar
130g desiccated coconut
320g self raising flour
3 medium eggs beaten
1 teaspoon mixed spice

Preheat the oven to 160°C.

Melt the butter in a saucepan over low heat.

Mix all the ingredients into the butter.

Cook in a lined roasting tin/brownie pan for 25 minutes.

The trick is not to overcook, so take it out when you think it's not quite ready.

Chocolate Cake – my Favourite

This is a wonderful cake with which you can indulge yourself and have with a cup of tea in the afternoon, or serve as a pudding with some Jersey cream if you can get it, or lovely vanilla ice cream. It is more dense than a good old Victoria sandwich but having done so many chocolate cakes, this is definitely my favourite.

Preheat the oven to 180°C.

Butter and line a 24cm cake tin.

Melt the chocolate for the cake very slowly in a thick-based pan with the coffee – stirring constantly – you really don't want to burn the chocolate. Remove from the heat and leave to cool.

Beat together 65g of the caster sugar with the butter and then add the 3 egg yolks.

Separately whisk the egg whites until they are very still and fold in the 20g of extra sugar.

Stir the cooled chocolate mixture into the egg yolk, butter and sugar mixture.

Add the ground almonds and plain flour and make sure it is all stirred in.

Gently fold in the beaten egg white mixture.

For a 20cm cake

175g Bournville chocolate or similar
6 tablespoons freshly made good coffee
85g caster sugar
125g butter, softened
3 medium eggs, separated
50g ground almonds
50g plain flour

Icing
50g dark chocolate
1 tablespoon golden syrup
50g butter

Put the mixture into the prepared cake tin and bake in the oven for 25 minutes – test with a skewer and make sure it comes out clean. Cook for another 5 minutes if the cake needs it.

Cool in tin for 15 minutes before turning it out on to a rack to cool.

To make the icing just melt the chocolate, golden syrup and butter together in a pan over a gentle heat.

Pour the icing over the cooled cake.

Chocolate Florentines

This is another of my all-time favourites and we have served these with coffee at so many weddings we have catered for, and they always get a mention in our thank-you letter. This recipe is for Di Clarfelt, who has always loved my take on these little gems.

Makes about 30

Preheat the oven to 170°C.

Combine sultanas, cornflakes, nuts, cherries and milk in large bowl.

Drop rounded teaspoons of mixture about 2cm apart on oven trays lined with baking paper.

Bake in oven for about 10 minutes or until browned.

Cool on trays.

Using a paint brush, paint the base of each Florentine with a thin layer of chocolate.

Lay on baking paper to dry.

80g sultanas
60g cornflakes
105g slivered almonds
105g glace cherries
160ml sweetened condensed milk
250g dark chocolate, melted

Coconut Cake with Coconut Icing

I absolutely love anything with coconut, especially puddings and cakes. Bounty Bars were always my favourite as a child! This recipe is for Mike Potter who, like me, always enjoys something sweet made with coconut.

Serves 8 – depending on how greedy!

275g plain flour
1 teaspoon baking powder
½ teaspoon bicarbonate of soda
½ teaspoon salt
275g butter, softened
300g caster sugar
4 medium eggs
½ teaspoon good almond essence
175ml full-fat milk
90g desiccated coconut

Icing
500g cream cheese
250g butter, softened at room temperature
½ teaspoon vanilla essence
500g sifted icing sugar
175g desiccated coconut

Preheat the oven to 170°C.

Butter and line two 24cm loose-bottomed cake tins.

Sift together the flour, baking powder, bicarbonate of soda and salt.

Beat the softened butter and sugar with an electric mixer until soft and light and then beat in the eggs, flour and almond essence.

Add the milk and the desiccated coconut.

Divide the mixture between the 2 cake tins and bake in the oven until firm to the touch – about 40 minutes. Do the skewer test again and if it comes out clean the cakes are ready.

Leave to cool in the tins for 10 minutes and then turn out onto a rack to cool.

Icing Beat gently by hand the butter, cream cheese and vanilla essence – do not use an electric whisk as it is too easy to over-beat.

Then gently fold in the sifted icing sugar – again don't over-beat.

Add 100g of the desiccated coconut and then spread half the icing over one cake – top with the other cake layer and spread the rest of the icing over the top.

Sprinkle the remaining coconut to decorate.

Homemade Granola

This is so easy to make – once you have made your own you will wonder how they charge so much for small packets in the shops.

Serves about 20

350g really good runny honey
225ml sunflower oil
300g bran flakes
200g wheat flakes
150g sultanas
150g roasted hazelnuts, halved
25g sunflower seeds, roasted
50g dried apricots, chopped
50g dates, chopped
75g wheat germ

Preheat the oven to 180°C.

Get yourself a large saucepan and melt the honey and sunflower oil together, then add the bran and wheat flakes.

When well covered in the oil and honey, pour the bran and wheat flakes onto 1 or 2 large baking sheets covered in non-stick paper.

Bake for 25 minutes – turning halfway through. Once toasted take out of the oven to cool and then mix in the sultanas and the rest of the ingredients.

Keep in a screw topped jar or airtight container for a couple of weeks.

Homemade Muesli

This is also easy to make – you just have to get the right ingredients. They don't all have to be exact – you could use any nuts instead of hazelnuts. Equally you can use any dried fruit of your choice.

Makes about 500g

250g bran flakes or wheat flakes
25g wheat bran
20g sesame seeds
60g sunflower seeds
10g linseeds
60g hazelnuts or walnuts
60g dried sour cherries
2 tablespoons sultanas

Preheat the oven to 180°C.

Put all the flakes and seeds in a roasting pan and bake for about 15 minutes – keeping an eye on them.

Roughly chop the nuts and put them in the baking tin for the last few minutes.

Keep in airtight container for up to 2 weeks.

Eat with cold milk – it is especially good with oat milk.

Kolakakor or Golden Syrup Biscuits

Delicious little biscuits which my friend, Lu Bevan, gave me the recipe for. They always work and are very easy.

Makes about 40

360g plain flour
2 teaspoons baking powder
1 vanilla pod or 2 drops of good vanilla essence
200g soft butter, diced
200g caster sugar
90g golden syrup

Preheat the oven to 180°C.

Sift the flour and baking powder into a bowl.

Slit the vanilla pod lengthways, scrape out the seeds and mix them into the flour.

Add all the rest of the ingredients and mix well until you have a firm, smooth paste – this can be done by hand or in a food mixer.

Divide the mixture into four pieces and roll out each one to 25cm long and 2.5cm thick.

Place on a baking tray lined with baking parchment, making sure they are at least 10cm apart as they will spread out in the oven.

Bake for 25–30 minutes, until golden brown.

When they come out of the oven, leave for two minutes, then cut each piece into 10 strips. Great served with ice cream, cream desserts or just a mug of tea.

Lemon Drizzle Cake (Auntie Judy)

Another one of my old-fashioned comforting recipes – it is lovely with a cup of tea! I found this in my mother's old recipe book, all handwritten and sent to her by her old school friend, Judy. If they were still alive, they would both be pushing 100 years old. This was sent to her in the 70s – I had no idea lemon drizzle cake had been around for so long!

Preheat the oven to 150°C.

Beat together the butter and sugar until pale and creamy, then add the eggs one at a time, slowly mixing through.

Sift in the flour, then add the lemon zest and milk and mix until well combined.

Line a loaf tin (8 x 21cm) with non-stick baking paper, then spoon in the mixture and level the top with a spoon.

Bake for 45–50 minutes until a thin skewer inserted into the centre of the cake comes out clean.

While the cake is cooling in its tin, mix together the lemon juice and icing sugar to make the drizzle.

Prick the warm cake all over with a skewer or fork, then pour over the drizzle – the juice will sink in and the sugar will form a lovely, crisp topping.

Leave in the tin until completely cool, then remove and serve.

Tip Will keep in an airtight container for 3–4 days or freeze for up to 1 month.

For the cake
225g butter, softened
225g caster sugar
4 eggs
zest of 2 lemons
225g self raising flour
1 tablespoon milk

For the drizzle topping
juice of 2 lemons
85g icing sugar, sieved

Perfect Chocolate Brownies

We have tried so many chocolate brownie recipes in my time. So much so, we had a whole day with my lovely chef, Nat, trying all sorts of different variations, and this we feel is the best. It always works for us.
I don't use 70% cocoa chocolate as I find it too bitter. As I have said before, I love eating it on its own but don't really enjoy cooking with it. I recommend buying good quality dark chocolate with a minimum 54% cocoa solids.

Makes 12

150g butter, chopped in small pieces
300g dark chocolate, broken into small pieces
330g light soft brown sugar
4 medium eggs, beaten
100g plain flour or ground almonds
120g sour cream or crème fraîche
75g walnuts or hazelnuts (optional)
pinch sea salt

Preheat the oven to 175°C.

Grease and line a 20 x 30cm tin with non-stick baking paper.

Stir the butter and chocolate in a heavy pan over a very low heat until smooth and melted.

Transfer chocolate mixture to a medium bowl and stir in the sugar, eggs, flour, sour cream and nuts – mix well and pour into prepared tin.

Bake uncovered in the oven for about 30 minutes until cooked. Cool in the pan.

Pistachio Cake

You can either bake this in a round 24cm loose-bottomed cake tin or make it in a loaf tin – I prefer the cake tin. I love this recipe but then I do love anything with pistachios.

Serves 8

250g softened butter
225g caster sugar
zest of 1 lemon
4 medium eggs
50g plain flour
100g ground almonds
100g ground pistachios
1 teaspoon baking powder
pinch sea salt

Preheat the oven to 170°C.

Line whichever tin you are going to use with greaseproof paper.

Beat the softened butter with the caster sugar until a light colour and then add the eggs one at a time – don't worry if it slightly curdles. Just gently fold in the flour, ground almonds and pistachios, baking powder and sea salt.

Bake in the oven for 35 minutes – test with a skewer and if it does not come out clean, cook for a further 5 minutes.

Leave it to cool in the tin and then turn out onto a wire rack.

Tip Simply sprinkle with some icing sugar before serving.

Shortbread

This really is a very good shortbread recipe – serve it mid-morning with a cup of coffee or mid-afternoon with a lovely cup of tea. You could add some grated lemon or orange zest to the mixture before cooking. You could also serve it beside a delicious little lemon posset as a pudding or a panna cotta.

Makes 12 pieces

- 250g butter (plus extra for greasing)
- 125g caster sugar (plus extra for sprinkling)
- 250g plain flour, sifted (plus extra for dusting)
- 125g semolina or cornflour

Preheat the oven to 140°C.

Grease a 22cm square tin.

Cream the butter and sugar with a whisk or wooden spoon until pale, light and fluffy.

Add the flour and semolina or cornflour. Mix very lightly with a wooden spoon, then with your hands until it's a smooth dough.

Transfer to a floured surface and roll out to 2cm thick. Press into the tin, poking into the corners with your fingers.

Prick all over with a fork, then bake for 50 minutes until lightly golden.

Sprinkle generously with caster sugar while still warm, then cool slightly and cut into 12 pieces.

Soda Bread

This is from a friend of mine, Nick Goldsmid. It is so good and always works a treat – it also freezes well. I make one loaf, slice it and put it in the freezer and then can just take out a slice when I need it and it makes wonderful toast for breakfast.

Makes 1 loaf

- 350g plain flour, plus extra for dusting
- 150g wholemeal flour
- 1½ teaspoons bicarbonate of soda
- 1 teaspoon table salt
- 1 teaspoon caster sugar
- 350ml buttermilk (if you do not have buttermilk, use skimmed milk and add 1½ teaspoons of cream of tartar instead)

Preheat the oven to 220°C.

Put the dry ingredients into a bowl and make a well in the middle. Reserve a third of the buttermilk and add the rest to the bowl, mixing lightly with a fork as you add it. Be careful not to over-work the dough but make sure all the dry ingredients are mixed in.

Add the remaining buttermilk.

Tip the dough on to a floured work surface and gently bring it all together to combine. Do not over-work.

Take a baking sheet and dust with flour.

Form the bread into a round, place on the sheet.

Use a serrated knife to cut a deep cross in the top of the loaf.

Place in the oven and bake for 10 minutes and then turn the heat down to 200°C and cook for another 25 minutes until the soda bread is golden on the outside and cooked through. A good way to check is by tapping the base – it should sound hollow when cooked.

Cool on a wire rack before enjoying warm or cold.

Tip Also, add seeds or any flavourings you like into the mix. You can also use these to decorate the top.

Vegan Chocolate Brownies

A favourite choice of pudding at the weddings we do is salted caramel chocolate brownies. Nowadays we always have a few vegan and dairy-free guests, so we have designed the recipe below for them and it is actually very nice.

Makes 12

200g ground almonds
100g ground walnuts
50g chopped pecans
7 tablespoons of raw cacao powder
200g soft stoned dates
75g runny honey
zest of 1 large orange
pinch of sea salt

Put everything apart from the chopped pecans into a food processor until well mixed.

Push the mixture into a lined brownie tin, sprinkle over the chopped pecans and leave in the fridge until set.

Cut into squares.

Basic Victoria Sandwich Cake Recipe

Once you have mastered this recipe which is incredibly easy, you can cook any flavour of cake you like. The recipe below is for a plain vanilla Victoria sponge but you could add any of the flavourings I list below for a different flavour.

Preheat the oven to 160°C.

Butter 2 x 20cm cake tins.

I just put the whole lot in an electric mixer or a bowl and use an electric hand whisk and whisk until the mixture is light and fluffy.

250g Flora or softened butter
250g caster sugar
250g self raising flour
4 large eggs
a few drops of natural vanilla essence

Transfer equally to the two cake tins and put in the oven for 25 minutes until it is cooked – test with a skewer as I have mentioned before and if it comes out clean then the cake is cooked.

With a vanilla cake I sandwich it together with some raspberry jam and some butter icing.

For a chocolate cake, reduce the flour by 25g and replace with cocoa powder.

For a coffee cake, add 2 tablespoons of strong freshly brewed coffee to the cake mixture.

For a lemon cake, add the zest of 2 lemons to the cake mixture.

See next page for icing recipes.

Cakes & Baking

Butter icing

Beat the butter in a large bowl until soft and then add half the icing sugar and beat until smooth.

Add the remaining icing sugar, the milk and the vanilla and beat the mixture until creamy and soft.

Add a bit more milk if necessary.

140g softened butter
280g icing sugar, sifted
1 tablespoon milk
¼ teaspoon vanilla extract

Lemon version

Add juice of 2 lemons to the buttercream.

Chocolate version

Add 75g melted dark chocolate to the buttercream.

Coffee version

Add a tablespoon of strong coffee to the buttercream.

Best-ever Chocolate Icing

This is so delicious and wonderful for topping a lovely chocolate cake – it is the best. You can let It go hard and cold in a fridge and then roll it into chocolate truffles, which you dust in cocoa powder if you like.

360g Bournville chocolate or equivalent
250g butter
2 tablespoons golden syrup

Literally all you do is slowly melt the lot in a small heavy pan and then stir until well mixed.

Once cooled a bit, pour it over your chosen cake!

Lovely Gluten-Free Bread

This is the only gluten-free bread recipe I have found which is really very good. Not that cheap to buy all the ingredients, but once you have them it is easy to do. It also freezes really well. Francesca Fabian, who works for me, gave me this recipe and I am so grateful to her as I had given up on finding an edible gluten-free bread recipe.

Makes 1 loaf

135g sunflower seeds
90g flax seeds
65g hazelnuts or almonds
145g rolled oats
2 tablespoons chia seeds
4 tablespoons psyllium husks or 3 tablespoons of the powder
½ teaspoon sea salt
1 tablespoon maple syrup
3 tablespoons coconut oil
350ml water

Use a loaf tin, put all the dry ingredients into it and give them a good mix.

Combine the oil, maple syrup and water together and mix into the dry ingredients – work it into a soft dough – if you need a bit more water then add another tablespoon.

Flatten the top and then leave it out for a minimum of 2 hours or up to 12 hours until the dough will be ready to bake.

Preheat the oven to 175°C.

Put the tin in the oven for 20 minutes – take it out of the oven and remove the loaf from the tin.

Put the loaf back into the oven and bake for a further 40 minutes.

The bread is ready when it sounds hollow when you tap it. Leave it to cool completely until you slice it.

Carrot Cake

I love carrot cake – so easy to make and for some reason people think it is healthy, but once you look at the ingredients you will realise it isn't! The combination of the cake with the cream cheese icing – really yummy.

Serves 8

The cake
200g plain flour
3 teaspoons baking powder
3 teaspoons ground cinnamon
½ teaspoon salt
100g sultanas
100g pecan pieces
200g carrots, grated
zest of 1 orange
3 large eggs, beaten
250g light soft brown sugar
250ml sunflower oil or 250g butter, melted

Cream cheese icing ingredients
100g icing sugar, sifted
200g full-fat cream cheese at room temperature
100g softened butter, room temp.

Preheat the oven to 170°C.

Grease a 26cm loose-bottomed cake tin and line with non-stick baking paper.

Sift together the plain flour, baking powder, cinnamon and salt.

Stir in the sultanas, grated carrot and nuts along with the orange zest.

Whisk the light brown sugar with the eggs until light and fluffy and then stir in the sunflower oil or butter.

Then add this mixture to the carrot mixture and put it all in the cake tin. Bake until you test it with a skewer and it comes out clean – about 50 minutes.

Let it cool in the tin for 15 minutes or so and then turn onto a rack to cool completely before covering it in the icing.

Cream cheese icing This can easily go wrong if you overbeat the cream cheese and butter. Don't be put off by this – just don't beat too much!

Sieve the icing sugar into a large bowl.

Place the softened butter and cream cheese into the middle of the bowl and beat gently with an electric mixer – keep the speed to 1 if possible and stop once it is all mixed. If you over-beat it will all separate.

Auntie Kay's Scones

Sorry to keep bringing things back to my family, but we are a family of food-lovers so it is nice to be reminded of favourite people who used to bake for us. Auntie Kay lived in a house right opposite the Sea View Hotel in the Isle of Wight and knew everyone there. I used to go and stay with her lots, and when we arrived, she would either have baked us a Victoria sandwich cake with jam and buttercream in the middle or scones, which she always served with Jersey butter and her homemade strawberry jam – gosh they were so good. Here is her recipe.

Makes 10

Preheat the oven to 220°C.

Auntie Kay would mix the fat, flour, sugar and salt together in a bowl with her fingertips until it resembled fine breadcrumbs and then add 1 tablespoon buttermilk and the beaten egg.

Bring it all together to a dough with a palette knife.

Once the dough is formed, roll it out on a floured surface – to at least 2.5cm thick.

Stamp into rounds with a 5cm cutter.

Place the scones on a greased baking tray and brush them lightly with the remaining buttermilk.

Bake in the preheated oven for 10–12 minutes until they are well risen and golden brown.

225g self raising flour
75g butter
40g caster sugar
¼ teaspoon salt
1 large egg, beaten
2 tablespoons buttermilk or sour cream

Shona's Flapjack

My mother used to make the best flapjacks ever and I have tried and tried to copy her and at last think I have managed to get the recipe as she used to do it – I think the trick is to add a couple of tablespoons of flour to the recipe which helps make the flapjacks a bit chewy and not too crumbly.

Makes about 16 squares

225g butter or margarine, melted
8 level tablespoons golden syrup
325g rolled oats
100g desiccated coconut
25g plain flour
½ teaspoon salt

Preheat the oven to 160°C.

33 x 21cm brownie tin lined with non-stick paper.

All you have to do is melt the margarine ("marge" as my mother called it) or butter in a heavy saucepan along with the golden syrup.

Then just stir in the oats, coconut, flour and salt and stir well.

Put the mixture into the prepared brownie tin and cook for 35 minutes until nice and brown on top.

Take out of the oven and leave to cool in the tin, but cut into 16 or so squares straight away – if you leave the flapjacks to cool in the tin they will go too hard and crisp and break into small pieces when you try and cut them.

Cakes & Baking

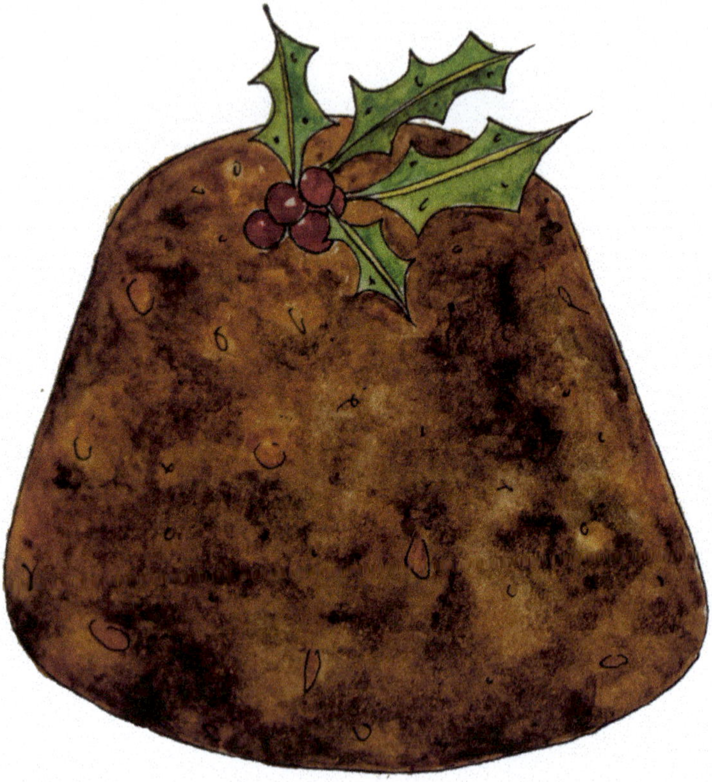

Christmas

Auntie Kay's Christmas Cake

In this Christmas section I am afraid there are a few Christmas cakes for you to choose from – as this book started off as a selection of recipes for my family, I have included all of them and hope you enjoy them too. My family have always been great bakers and my late aunt from the Isle of Wight loved making us a Christmas cake every year; below is the recipe.

350g plain flour
½ teaspoon mixed spice
½ teaspoon mace
½ teaspoon cinnamon
280g butter
280g demerara sugar
1 tablespoon black treacle
570g currants
350g raisins
350g sultanas
250ml brandy or sherry
115g blanched almonds, chopped
115g glace cherries, chopped
grated zest of 1 lemon
grated zest of 1 orange
170g mixed crystallised peel
pinch of salt
5 medium eggs, beaten

Preheat the oven to 150°C.

Line a 22cm, 2.5cm deep cake tin with two layers of non-stick paper and cover the outside of the tin with brown paper.

Soak all dried fruit in the brandy or sherry.

Beat butter and sugar with treacle until fluffy.

Add beaten eggs and flour gently into the beaten butter and sugar.

Stir in the spices and spoon in the soaked dried fruit, zests, glace cherries, crystallised peel and salt.

Add the blanched almonds.

Put the cake mixture in the tin and top with more non-stick paper.

Bake for 1½ hours at 150°C and then 2½ hours at 140°C.

Auntie Kay's Christmas Pudding

Another classic recipe from my wonderful Auntie Kay. She always used to arrive with this pudding, which she had lovingly made for us for Christmas and it was absolutely scrummy. I still have the cake tin she used to bring it in – a wonderful old thing, which I have marked not to throw out in my will!

Put all the ingredients together stirring well and leave for 24 hours – stirring occasionally (make a wish each time you stir – you can get all the family to have a stir and a wish).

Pour into a greased basin and cover with greaseproof paper and steam for approximately 6 hours.

Serves 8

125g stale white breadcrumbs
75g plain flour
125g demerara sugar
125g shredded suet (if you don't like using suet you could replace with grated butter)
500g mixed dried fruit (any will do)
1 level tablespoonful treacle or golden syrup
125g mixed peel
125g blanched almonds
1 small apple, grated
grated zest and juice of 1 lemon
1 small carrot, grated
1 teaspoon mixed spice
1 teaspoon cinnamon
½ teaspoon freshly grated nutmeg
1 egg, beaten
142ml of any of the following: ale, beer, stout, brandy, whisky or milk

Christmas Pudding

My father's recipe – it is as he wrote it, apart from the fact that I have had to update the measurements. I have left in the sentence about the money covered in foil and the Christmas charms, as it was so exciting for us to find them in the pudding and is such a nostalgic memory. With health and hygiene rules you probably are not allowed to do this anymore!

Serves 10–12

- 110g shredded suet or butter if you prefer not to use suet
- 50g self raising flour
- 110g white breadcrumbs
- 1 level teaspoon ground mixed spice
- ¼ teaspoon freshly grated nutmeg
- generous pinch of cinnamon
- 225g light soft brown sugar
- 110g sultanas
- 110g raisins
- 275g currants
- 25g mixed candied peel, finely chopped
- 25g almonds, skinned and chopped
- 1 small cooking apple, peeled, cored and grated
- zest of 1 orange
- zest of 1 lemon
- 2 medium eggs
- 75ml barley wine
- 75ml stout
- 2 tablespoons rum

You will need a 1.2 litre (2-pint) pudding basin, lightly greased with butter.

Begin the day before you want to steam the pudding. In the largest bowl possible, put the suet, flour, breadcrumbs, spices and sugar.

Mix all these together and add the dried fruits, mixed peel, nuts, apple and fruit zest.

Mix the eggs and liquid ingredients together and pour into the fruit mixture, mixing thoroughly. It should be a sloppy mixture. If too dry, add a bit more stout.

Stir in your money covered in foil or Christmas charms.

Cover the bowl and leave overnight.

The next day pack the mixture into the bowl and cover with a double sheet of greaseproof paper and a sheet of foil. Tie it securely with string – tightly!

Tie a piece of string across the top to make a handle.

Put the bowl in a large pan of simmering water so it comes halfway up the sides of the bowl and steam for 6 hours, checking regularly to see there is sufficient water in the pan. Top up with water from a boiling kettle.

Leave the pudding to get cold and then remove the steaming foil and paper and replace with fresh paper and foil. Secure tightly.

Keep in a cool place out of the light.

Aga cooks can steam puddings in the simmering oven according to the Aga Cook Book instructions.

On Christmas Day the pudding needs to be steamed for about 2 hours. It should be delicious with your brandy/rum butter.

Dad Baker's Christmas Pudding (1968)

This is the recipe my father and stepmother made every year – I think it was originally from the Daily Mirror. *This is in the book for Alexander, my lovely nephew, who always reminds me of my father.*

450g currants
450g sultanas
450g raisins
110g mixed peel
110g chopped glace cherries
75g chopped almonds
50g ground almonds
350g light soft brown sugar
1½ teaspoons of mixed spice
1 teaspoon freshly grated nutmeg
juice and peel of one lemon
250ml rum
250ml brandy
8 eggs, well beaten
450g breadcrumbs
200g flour
pinch of salt
200g suet
spoonful of butter

Mix the dried fruit, peel, cherries, almonds, sugar, spices and lemon juice with the brandy and rum and leave in a covered bowl for at least three days.

After three days, add the beaten eggs.

Then add the breadcrumbs, flour, pinch of salt and suet. Give it a really thorough stir.

When the above is done, butter and flour three bowls and three-quarters fill them with the mixture.

Cover the bowls with buttered greaseproof paper and a sheet of foil, tied securely with string.

Steam for 6 hours minimum.

Dad Baker's Christmas Cake

This one is for my brother, Jono, who always loves a Christmas cake. Another recipe more to amuse my family than anyone else! In 1972 this cost Dad 64½ pence and, in 1973, 73½ pence!

Preheat the oven to 140°C.

Line a 22cm deep tin with a double layer of buttered greaseproof paper.

Beat butter to a cream and then add the sugar until soft and fluffy.

Fold in 2 tablespoons of flour.

Add the eggs one at a time, beating between each addition.

Mix together the dried fruit, cherries, peel, lemon zest and almonds and add to the egg and butter mixture.

Add the remainder of the flour and stir until all is well mixed and the fruit is well distributed.

Add the lemon juice and bandy and stir in well.

Transfer to the tin and cook for about 5 hours.

225g plain flour
225g light soft brown sugar
225g butter
350g currants
350g sultanas
350g deseeded raisins
110g glace cherries
175g mixed peel
50g sweet almonds
25g bitter almonds
200ml brandy
5 eggs
¼ teaspoon freshly grated nutmeg
1 teaspoon mixed spice
pinch of ground mace
pinch of salt
zest and juice of 1 lemon

Shona's Christmas Pudding

I have tried so many versions of Christmas puddings and so many are good, but this is the recipe I have created for a large 2kg cake and I think it is brilliant. It is delicious and so easy to make, so here goes.

Serves 10

250g butter or Flora
250g light soft brown sugar
200g self raising flour
4 eggs
1½ teaspoons freshly grated nutmeg
1 teaspoon allspice
½ teaspoon ground cinnamon
250g sultanas
250g raisins
125g dried apricots, chopped, or mixed peel, chopped
250g currants
125g almonds, chopped
500g apples, grated (leave the skin on before grating)
zest and juice of 1 orange and 1 lemon
6 tablespoons brandy or rum or Guinness

Put the dried fruit, chopped almonds, grated apple, orange juice and lemon juice and zest in a large bowl and pour over the brandy, rum or Guinness. Give it a good stir.

If you have an electric mixer just put the softened butter or Flora, sugar, self raising flour, spices and eggs into the mixer and beat until soft and creamy.

Just mix the dried fruit mixture with the creamed butter, sugar, eggs and flour mixture and put into a greased pudding bowl – grease with some softened butter.

Cover with some non-stick paper and cover with tin foil which must be tied with string around the rim.

Put the bowl in a large pan on a trivet or just some folded tin foil and steam in a large pan for about 4 hours – so many recipes say 6–8 hours but I think you end up with a bullet of Christmas pudding. Don't forget to keep filling the pan up with water – the water should come halfway up the pudding bowl and always keep a lid on the saucepan.

Sage, Leek & Onion Balls

These are perfect made in advance and frozen for Christmas or any roast chicken Sunday lunch – they are so good and heat up again very well after freezing. I will always think of my lovely chef, Paul Boarder, when I do these as he always made them when we used to do the London Rowing Club annual dinner for members in December.

Makes 18

4 tablespoons sunflower oil
2 onions, finely chopped
1 leek, finely sliced
2 celery sticks, finely chopped
450g good quality pork sausages, meat squeezed out
20g fresh sage leaves, finely chopped
140g white breadcrumbs
1 large egg
8 smoked dry-cured streaky bacon rashers, halved and stretched out

Preheat the oven to 180°C.

Heat the oil in a large frying pan; soften the onions, leek and celery for 15 minutes.

Put the sausage meat into a bowl.

Once the onion mix has cooled, tip onto the sausage meat, add the sage, bread, egg and some seasoning. Then mix really well with your hands.

Shape into little golf-ball-sized spheres and wrap each in the stretched bacon.

Put them on a baking sheet lined with baking paper and cover with foil.

Bake for 15 minutes and then take the foil off and bake for another 30 minutes until the bacon is golden.

Cranberry & Orange Relish

A delicious and easy way to make cranberry sauce for Christmas. Claire Allen gave me this recipe years ago and I have done it every Christmas since.

Serves 12

675g fresh cranberries
zest and juice of 2 medium oranges
6cm cinnamon stick
6 cloves
115g caster sugar
5 tablespoons port

Chop the cranberries up in a food processor and place them in a saucepan.

Add the orange zest and juice to the pan with the cinnamon, cloves and sugar. Bring to simmering point and cover with a lid.

Simmer very gently for about 5 minutes.

Remove from the heat and stir in the port. Leave to cool.

Tip This freezes very well and should be defrosted before serving at room temperature. Don't forget to remove the cinnamon and cloves!

Delicious Drinks

Cranberry Cooler

Pour all ingredients together and serve cooled.

1 litre cranberry juice
1 litre orange juice
ice cubes
1 litre sparkling mineral water
twists of orange peels

Rock Shandy

Fill glass with ice cubes and sparkling water, add sprig of mint and half a teaspoon Angostura bitters. Do not stir.

1 litre sparkling mineral water
Angostura bitters
ice cubes
sprigs fresh mint

Sloe Gin (Auntie Kay's recipe)

I am sure everyone has this recipe, but I have to include it, in memory of my wonderful Auntie Kay who just loved nature and lived on the Isle of Wight. She always made her own sloe gin every year and probably drunk the lot with her best friend Marjorie, who lived next door! As you will have noticed, a few of her recipes appear in this book!

Wash and prick the sloes.

Put all ingredients into a large bottle and shake every day until the sugar has melted.

1kg sloes, picked in September
125g demerara sugar
6 almonds, blanched
1 litre gin

Store in a cool, dry place for a minimum of 18 months.

Line a sieve with a square of muslin and drain into a large bowl.

Decant the gin into clean, dry bottles.

Keeps forever!

Auntie Nan's Punch

This is a wonderful winter punch and I got the recipe from my Auntie Nan, my father's sister, who was a fabulous lady. Great to take in a flask on a shoot or at a rugby match picnic. It is pretty strong so you would not need much!

Makes 1.5 litres

500ml hot China tea
250ml pint brandy
250ml Jamaica rum
1 small wine glass of Grand Marnier
1 small wine glass green Chartreuse
juice of 2 limes
thin slice of lemon
sugar to taste

Mix all ingredients in a large saucepan and bring to the boil.

Serve hot.

Acknowledgements

I have so many people to thank.

My wonderful PA, Emily Hill. Without her I would not have known how to get started and she has encouraged and helped me all along the way.

A huge thank you to Alex Walters, my marvellous therapist, who told me to stop knocking myself and get on with it. He taught me to believe in myself, be positive and to put all my positive energy into writing *Muddy Spuds*.

Sam, at Tandem Publishing, who has done so much work helping me create this book.

Thank you to Harriet Hodgkinson for the beautiful illustrations she has provided for the cover and interior.

Mark Hodgkinson's wonderful photography captures my love of colourful, fresh ingredients and helped me feel comfortable in front of the camera – no mean feat! I would like to thank him for so generously spending an afternoon with me in my kitchen.

To my eccentric family who all love my food and with whom I talk about food all the time; especially my sister Nicky who I probably share recipes with most days if not certainly 2 or 3 times a week. A huge thank you to my father who would be 101 should he still be alive – he introduced me to the love of really good, seasonal food and he only settled for the best. He never kept quiet in some of London's best restaurants if he felt the food was not up to standard! He was amongst the first to send in write ups to the "Good Food Guide" and was quoted so often.

Thank you to my husband, Ronnie, for putting up with me during Covid lockdown – he helped me with my catering business, which completely changed over the last year, and has been so supportive and encouraging about my venture into writing this book.

Thank you to my tolerant, funny and friendly team – Paul, Liz, Nat, Wiz, Mary and Bridie and many others who have made my catering life so fun and rewarding. Without them I would have given up years ago.

Thank you to my wonderful clients, for whom I have cooked for so many years. Their encouragement and excitement about the book has helped me so much.

To my son, Max, who has inspired me in his route to recovery from addiction. It was whilst he was away in South Africa in rehab that I started writing the book to take my whirring, worrying mind off thinking about him all the time. He is a brilliant chef and artist and I like to think that he will now have a book of all our family recipes to keep with him and to hand on to any family he may have in the future.

Suppliers

Mackens Butcher
44 Turnham Green Terrace, Chiswick, London W4 1QP
020 8994 2646
Great butcher in Chiswick, run and owned by Rodney who delivers all around London. Great meat at great prices and it is a lovely shop to visit – all beautifully laid out.

Barnes Fish Shop
18 Barnes High Street, Barnes, London SW13 9LD
0208 876 1297
Lovely fresh fish shop in Barnes High Street run and owned by Michael. Delicious fresh fish each day and he will deliver to you in London as well.

Two Peas In A Pod
85 Church Road, Barnes, London SW13 9HH
020 8748 0232
Run and owned by Malcolm – full of wonderful, interesting produce, which he will deliver if you order in advance.

Persian Food Shop
Suroor
101 Robin Hood Way, Kingston Vale, London SW15 3QE
020 8974 6088
This really is worth a visit. Excellent and very reasonably priced fresh vegetables and fruit – super mangoes – the best I have found in London. Their butcher is also first rate and I buy great shoulders of lamb, which I slow-cook using their huge bunches of fresh herbs. Their lemons are just like the ones I have come across in Greece in the summer.

Asian Food Shop
Thai Smile Supermarket
283-287 King Street, Hammersmith, London W6 9NH
020 8846 9960
A fantastic selection of anything Asian you might like to buy – huge bottles of soy sauce, sesame oil and fish sauce and excellent Thai curry pastes etc.

Barnes Cheese Shop
62 Barnes High Street, Barnes, London SW13 9LF
020 8878 6676
A super little cheese shop in Barnes High Street where I always buy the cheese we need for weddings. They have never let me down – they know so much about all different types of cheeses and are experts at storing them properly.

Index

Alaska Crumble Pie 211
ale 143, 285
Almond, Polenta & Lemon Cake 253
Almond Tart 212
almonds 231, 263, 277, 286, 288-290
   blanched 284-285, 293
   flaked 255-256
   ground 212, 227, 233, 251-253, 255, 261, 270-271, 274, 288
amaretti biscuits 225, 254
Angostura bitters 293
Apple & Amaretti Tart 254
Apple Amber 213
apricots 8, 154, 212, 266, 290
Asian Slaw 74
Aubergine, Feta & Broad Bean Salad 78
Aubergine Parmigiana 192
aubergines 41, 52, 54, 78, 81, 149-150, 162, 192
avocados 15, 33, 40, 56, 67, 71, 202

Babotie 161
bacon 103, 174, 291
Bacon, Baked Canadian 132
Balsamic Dressing 188
bananas 241
barley wine 286
Béarnaise Sauce, Cheat's 168-169
beef 143-144, 152, 179
   brisket 163
   mince 149, 160, 165
   fillet 142, 168
   see also oxtail, steak, veal
Beef Brisket with Red Wine & Thyme 163-164
Beef, Carbonnade of 143
Beef Stroganoff 142
Beef with Chilli & Coriander Dressing 148
beer 285

beetroot 21, 71
blackcurrants 214
Blinis 2
blue cheese 193-194, 200
Blue Cheese & Spinach Tart with Caramelised Onions 193-194
blueberries 211, 215, 232, 235, 250
Blueberry, Coconut & Lime Ice-Cream 215
Bolognese 160
brandy 18, 218, 284-285, 287-290, 294
Bread, Gluten-Free 277
Briam 52
broad beans 3-4, 78
broccoli 127, 137, 196
Brûlée, Spiced Tropical 241
Bruschetta with Broad Beans, Pecorino & Mint Oil 3-4
bulgur wheat 53, 63, 66, 84, 123, 128, 147, 154, 162
Bulgur Wheat with Pomegranates 53
butternut squash 64, 68, 201
Butternut Squash & Coconut Curry with Cashew Nuts 201

cabbage 74, 132, 172, 176, 203
cacao powder 274
Caesar Salad, Cheat's 56
Cake, Hunting 260
candied peel 286
capers 34, 54
Caponata 54
Carrot Cake 278
Carrots Vichy 55
cashews 8, 201
cauliflower 202, 207
Cauliflower & Potatoes with Indian Spices 207
celeriac 43, 68
Celeriac Remoulade with Serrano or

Parma Ham 43
celery 14, 44-45, 54, 75, 89, 94, 109, 136, 158, 160, 163, 179, 192, 198, 203, 291
Chartreuse 294
Chateaubriand with Béarnaise 168-169
cheddar 5, 12-13, 23-24, 127, 193, 196, 205
Cheese Aigrettes 5
Cheese Puffs 10
Cheese Soufflés, Double-Baked 23-24
Cheesecake, Orange & Yoghurt with Pistachios 222
Cheesecake, Simple 240
cherries
  dried 63, 172, 267
  glacé 218, 263, 284, 288-289
chia seeds 277
chicken 7, 14, 71, 75, 100-129, 177
Chicken & Lime Noodle Salad 126
Chicken & Walnut Sandwiches 14
Chicken Bake, Easy 127
Chicken Baked with Parmesan & Herbs 101-102
Chicken Bits with Thyme & Lemon 121
Chicken Chasseur 103
Chicken, Coronation 111
Chicken Curry 113
Chicken, Golden Jubilee 114
Chicken, Indonesian Marinated with Roast Sweet Potatoes & Peppers 115-116
Chicken, Leek & Tarragon Pie 104
chicken liver 18
Chicken Liver Pâté 18
Chicken, Malaysian 117-118
Chicken Marinade 105
Chicken, Marinated & Fried or Oven-Baked 125
Chicken, Mediterranean 119
Chicken, Moroccan 120
Chicken, Spiced with Feta & Herb Bulgur Wheat 128
Chicken, Sticky Thai 122
Chicken Stock xv, 75
Chicken Thighs, Barbecued 100

Chicken Thighs with Oregano & Pomegranate Molasses 106
Chicken, Wild Rice & Red Grape Salad 108
Chicken with Paprika, Cayenne Pepper & Thyme 112
Chicken with Yoghurt & Spices 107
Chicken, Zanzibar 124
chickpeas 73, 81, 201
Chickpeas with Aubergines & Tomatoes 81
chicory 138
Chilli Jam 185
Chocolate Biscuit Pudding Cake 218
Chocolate Brownies 270
Chocolate Brownies, Vegan 274
Chocolate Cake 261-262
Chocolate Florentines 263
Chocolate Mousse 234
Chocolate Pots 229
Chocolate Roulade 219
Chocolate Tart, Salted Caramel 238
Chocolate Truffles 220
Christmas Cake 284
Christmas Cake (Dad Baker) 289
Christmas Pudding 286-287
Christmas Pudding (Auntie Kay) 285
Christmas Pudding (Dad Baker) 288
Christmas Pudding (Shona) 290
cider 134, 136, 138, 158
Coconut Cake with Coconut Icing 264-265
coconut cream 215
coconut, desiccated 260, 264-265, 280
coconut milk 95, 97, 117-118, 124, 201
cod 85, 88-91, 97
Cod, Baked with Oregano & Lemon Potatoes 85
Cod, Butter Roasted with Spring Onion Mash 91
Coq au Vin Best Recipe 109-110
Cottage Pie 165-166
Courgette, Leek & Feta Frittata Canapés 11
Courgette Pasta 195

courgettes 11, 41, 52, 119, 195
crab 6, 40
Crab Cakes 6
Crab, Dill, Chives, Cucumber & Avocado Salad/Starter 40
cranberries 172, 292
Cranberry & Orange Relish 292
Cranberry Cooler 293
cream cheese 10, 19, 26-27, 37, 185, 240, 250, 264-265, 278
Crème Brûlée 221
Croque Monsieurs 13
Crumble 210
crystallised peel 284
cucumber 19-22, 25, 31, 34, 36-37, 40, 61, 72, 94
Cucumber & Cream Cheese Mousse 19-20
Cucumber & Yoghurt Soup for Summer 31
curd cheese 27

dates 242, 266, 274
Dauphinoise 57
Dhal 70
Dressing 189
Dressing, Simple 189
duck 172-173, 175, 178
Duck, Braised with Orange, Port & Dried Cherries 172-173
Duck Breasts with Pomegranate Molasses 175
Duck Legs, Slow-Cooked with Soy Ginger & Star Anise 178

Eton Mess 223

fennel 48, 60, 88
Fennel & Feta with Pomegranate Seeds & Sumac 60
Fennel & Mozzarella Salad 48
feta 11, 60-61, 69, 72-73, 78, 128, 198-199
Feta-Based Salads 72-73
Fish Curry, Massaman 97
Fish Curry, Tamarind 95

Fish Soup/Stew 89
Flapjack 280
flatbread 15, 81, 147, 167, 202, 206-207

gammon 132, 184
Gazpacho 25
gin 293
goat's cheese 26, 71
Goat's Cheese & Red Pepper Pâté 26
golden syrup 236, 261-262, 268, 276, 280, 285
gooseberries 224
Gooseberry Fool 224
Goulash 144
Grand Marnier 294
Granola, Homemade 266
grapes 71, 108, 176
Gratin Dauphinoise 58
green beans 28, 90, 117-118, 129, 155
Gruyère 5, 13, 23-24, 57-58, 193
guinea fowl 176-177
Guinea Fowl with Grapes & Port 176
Guinea Fowl with Peas & Pancetta 177
Guinness 290

haddock 84, 90, 97
Haddock with Herb & Walnut Crust 90
hake 88
haloumi 15
Haloumi & Avocado Bruschetta 15
ham 13, 184 *see also* Parma ham, Serrano ham
hazelnuts 176, 266-267, 270, 277

kale 45, 65, 67, 79, 203
Kale or Cavolo Nero, Roasted Crispy 65
Kale Pesto 79
Kale Salad 67
Kedgeree 84
Kolakakor or Golden Syrup Biscuits 268

lamb 144, 153-154
 fillet 146, 162, 167
 mince 147, 149, 161
 rack 151, 155-156

shoulder 145, 157
Lamb & Vegetable Stew 162
Lamb Cutlets with Sauce Paloise 155-156
Lamb in Coriander 146
Lamb Meatballs with Tahini 147
Lamb, Rack of with Orange, Honey & Soy 151
Lamb, Shoulder of 145
Lamb, Sweet Potato & Orzo Stew 167
Lamb, Wedding 157
leeks 11, 86, 89, 104, 136, 177, 291
Lemon Amaretti Cream Pots 225
Lemon Chiffon 226
lemon curd 216, 225, 227
Lemon Drizzle Cake 269
Lemon Meringue Pie 245-246
Lemon Posset with Lemon Shortbread 227-228
Lentil & Tomato Stew with Thyme & Kale or Cabbage 203
lychees 241

mango 74, 241
maple syrup 53, 277
Marsala 248
mascarpone cheese 193-194, 214, 222, 248
meringue 211, 213, 216, 223, 245-246
Meringue Recipe 216
monkfish 88-89, 92-93, 97
Monkfish with New Potatoes & Wilted Spinach 92-93
Moussaka 149-150
mozzarella 35, 44, 48, 192
Mozzarella with Toasted Ciabatta Sticks 44
Muesli, Homemade 267
Mushroom Pâté 27
Mushroom Risotto 197
mushrooms 27, 103, 109-110, 142, 197-198
Mustard Sauce 184

Nectarine Blueberry Crisp 232
nectarines 35, 214, 232

olives 32, 54, 61
Onions, Pickled 62
Orange & Almond Cake 233
Osso Buco Gremolata 158
oxtail 159
Oxtail, Slow-Cooked with Five Spice & Ginger 159

pancetta 45, 109-110, 136, 172, 177, 203
papaya 74
Parma ham 28, 38, 43
Parma Ham & Rocket Wraps 28
Parmesan 5, 10-12, 28, 32, 38, 45, 56, 58, 79-80, 101, 149-150, 192, 195, 197, 200, 205
Parmesan Biscuits 12
parsnips 68, 163, 178
passion fruit 241
Pastry, Easy Savoury 76
Pastry, Sweet Shortcrust 243
Pastry, Very Easy 77
Pea & Mint Soup 29
peaches 8, 214
Peaches (or Nectarines), Baked with Blackcurrants & Mascarpone & Crushed Digestives 214
peanut butter 201
Peanut Cakes, Crunchy Thai 7
peanuts 7
Pear & Ginger Tart 239
pears 212, 231, 236, 239
Pears, Poached with Fudge Sauce 236
Pears, Spiced 231
pecans 198, 274, 278
pecorino 3-4
peppers 25-26, 32, 41, 52, 61, 74, 115-116, 119, 126, 146, 162, 202
Pheasant Casserole 174
pheasants 174
physalis 241
pig's cheeks 136
Pig's Cheeks, Slow-Cooked 136
pine nuts 28, 32, 60, 64, 120, 123, 147, 154, 200
pineapple 241

Pistachio & Orange Tart 251-252
Pistachio Cake 271
Pistachio Ice Cream 235
pistachios 53, 63, 80, 108, 123, 154, 216, 222, 235
  ground 251-252, 271
plums 210
polenta 11, 253
pomegranate 53, 60, 63, 67, 107
pomegranate molasses 106, 175
pork 100, 133, 137-138, 144, 152-153
  mince 8, 149
  shoulder 134-135, 139
  see also bacon, gammon, pig's cheeks, sausages
Pork & Cashew Meatballs 8
Pork Belly, Roast 133
Pork Chops with Dijon Mustard & Cream 137
Pork Loin with Chicory & Cider 138
Pork, Shoulder of with Lemon & Chillies 135
Pork, Shoulder of with Prunes & Cider 134
Pork with Star Anise, Soy & Cinnamon 139
port 172, 176, 292
Potatoes with Lemon & Thyme 59
poussins 129
Poussins with Parsley, Chive & Thyme Sauce 129
Prawn & Caramelised Onion Pancakes 9
prawns 9, 89, 97
prosciutto 28
prunes 134, 218
psyllium husks 277
Punch 294
Puy Lentil & Kale Soup 45
Puy Lentil & Pecan Stew with Sweet Potatoes & Feta 198

Queen of Puddings 237
quinoa 53, 63
Quinoa, Camargue Red Rice, Pistachio & Dried Cherry Salad 63

raspberries 211, 223-224, 230, 250
Raspberry Jellies 230
ratafia biscuits 225
Red Onion Marmalade 187
Red Onions with Parma Ham, Rocket & Shaved Parmesan 38
redcurrants 211
rhubarb 217, 255
Rhubarb & Almond Cake with Flaked Almonds 255-256
Rhubarb Crumble Ice Cream, Cheat's 217
ricotta 41-42, 200
Rock Shandy 293
Rocket & Pistachio Pesto 80
Rocket, Chicken & Pistachio (or Pine Nut) Tabouli 123
rum 218, 286-288, 290, 294

Sage, Leek & Onion Balls 291
Sake 178
Salad, Greek 61
Salad Supper 71
salmon 21-22, 34, 46, 53, 86-87, 94-96
Salmon, Baked Parcels with Fresh Herbs 86-87
Salmon Rillettes with Bagel Toasts 46-47
salmon, smoked 2, 22, 36
Salmon, Smoked & Horseradish Creams 36
Salmon Starter with Sweet & Salted Cucumber with Dill 34
Salmon, Sumac & Citrus Baked 96
Salmon with Beetroot, Horseradish Cream & Pickled Cucumber 21-22
Salmon with Spring Onion Noodles 94
sausages 291
scallops 89
Scones 279
sea bass 33, 89
Sea Bass Ceviche with Avocado & Red Chilli 33
Seafood Provençal with Fennel 88
Serrano ham 43
sesame seeds 267
shallots 6, 46-47, 90, 109, 111, 117-118,

134, 138, 174, 177, 186
sherry 18, 132, 248, 284
Shortbread 272
shrimps 30
Shrimps, Potted 30
Sloe Gin 293
sloes 293
Soda Bread 273
Spaghetti Aglio e Olio 204
spinach 86, 92-93, 178, 193-194, 199-201, 206
Spinach & Feta Tart 199
Spinach & Lentil Dahl 206
Spinach & Ricotta Lasagne 200
spring onions 31, 34, 63, 72-73, 91, 94, 201
steak 143, 148, 160, 165, 168, 179
stout 285-286
strawberries 223-224
Summer Wedding Starter 35
sun-dried tomatoes 32
Sun-Dried Tomatoes with Red Peppers & Olives Mixture for Canapés 32
sunflower seeds 266-267, 277
swede 179
Sweet Potato Mash 68
Sweet Potato or Butternut Squash with Roasted Red Onion & Tahini 64
sweet potatoes 52, 64, 68, 115-116, 159, 162, 167, 196, 198, 206
swordfish 88

Tabouli 66
Tagine of Lamb with Mint, Apricots & Pine Nuts 154
Tarte Tatin 247
Tiramisu 248
Toffee, Sticky Pudding 242
Tomato Chutney, Green 186
Tomato Sauce with Baked Feta 69
Tomato Soup 39
Tomato Tart 205
treacle 284-285
Treacle Tart 244, 284-285
trout 37, 46

Trout, Smoked Pâté/Mousse 37
tuna 88
turnips 163, 179

veal 158
Vegetables, Roasted Mediterranean with Herb-Baked Ricotta 41-42
Vegetarian Goulash 202
Veggie Shepherd's Pie with Sweet Potato Mash 196
venison 179
Venison Stew with Redcurrant Jelly & Red Wine 179-180
Victoria Sandwich Cake Recipes 275-276
Vinaigrette 188

Walnut Shortbreads 249
walnuts 14, 31, 90, 96, 210, 216, 218, 242, 249, 267, 270, 274
whisky 285
White Chocolate & Blueberry or Raspberry Cheesecake 250
wine xv, 39, 88, 103, 109-111, 133, 137, 142, 149-150, 157, 160, 163-164, 174, 177, 179, 196, 230-231

yoghurt xv, 31, 53, 81, 107, 113, 115-116, 120, 157, 161, 167, 202, 207, 222-223, 225, 241

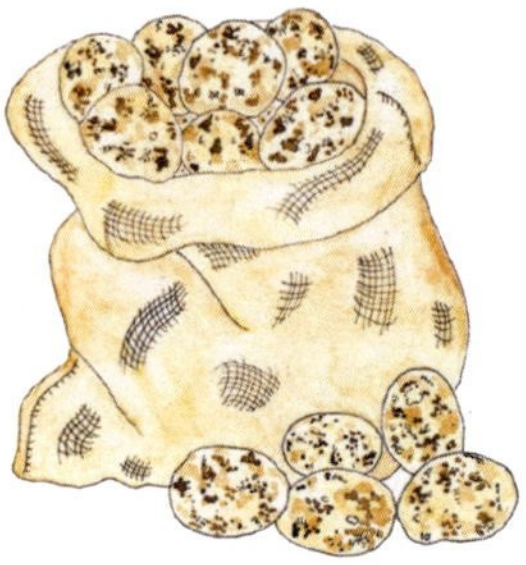
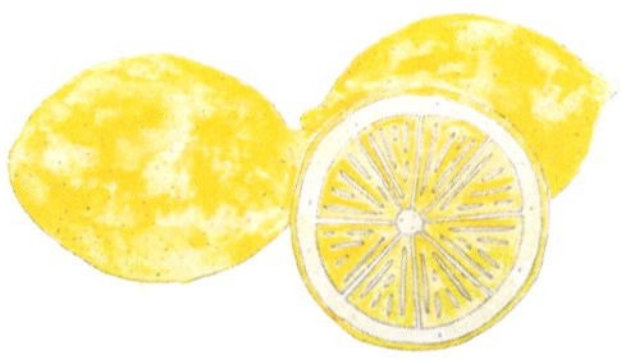
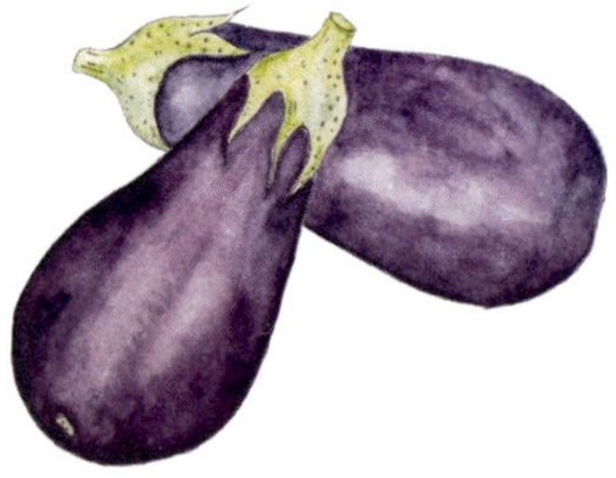
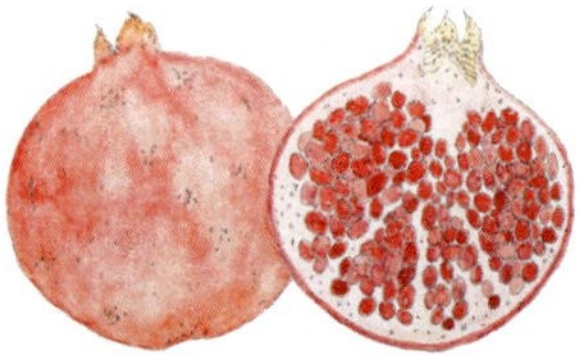
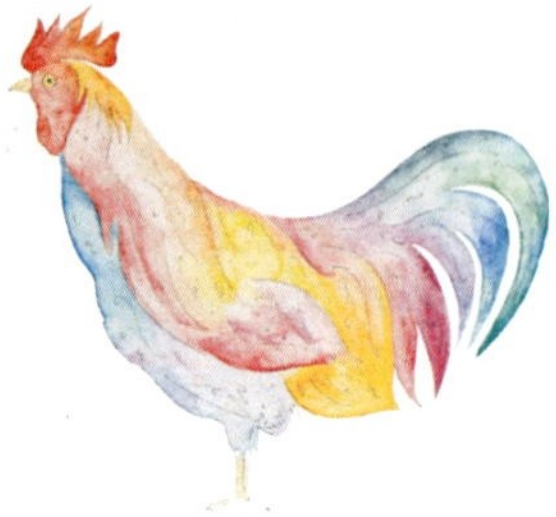
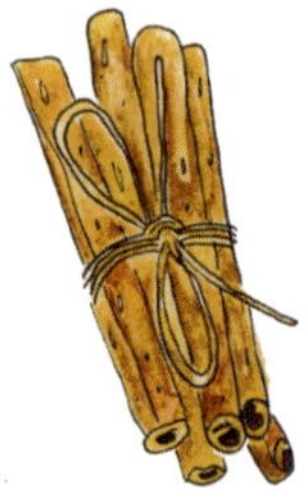
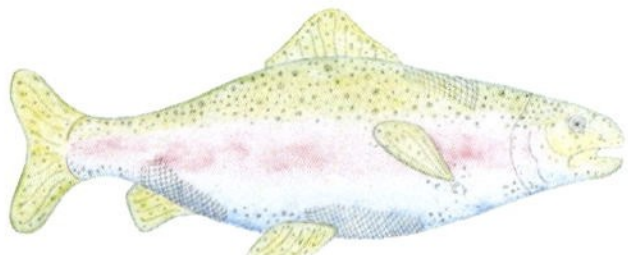
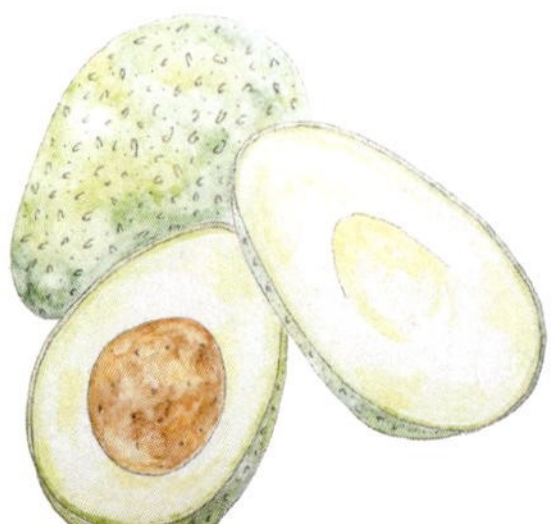
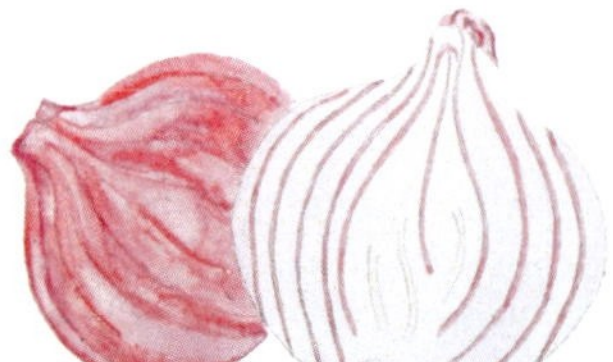